34
MOUNTAIN BIKE ROUTES
NORTHERN OREGON CASCADES

by

Don & Roberta Lowe

The Touchstone Press
Box 81
Beaverton, Oregon 97075

AGENCY LISTINGS

Listed below are addresses and phone numbers for the U.S. Forest Service Ranger Districts (all within the Mt. Hood National Forest) that have jurisdiction over 30 of the routes described in this guide. The relevant trip numbers are shown with each District. For those four not listed below, No. 4 is over a combination of State, BLM and private (with easements) lands, No. 29 is over Hood River County roads and No's. 30 and 31 are on Wasco County roads.

Mt. Hood National Forest
2955 N.W. Division Street
Gresham, Oregon 97030
666-0771

Columbia Gorge Ranger District 1, 2
31520 S.E. Woodard Road
Troutdale, Oregon 97060
695-2276

Zigzag Ranger District 3, 5, 6, 7, 8, 9
70220 E. Highway 26
Zigzag, Oregon 97049
666-0704 (from Portland)
622-3191 (other)

Bear Springs Ranger District .... 10, 11, 12, 15 (part of)
Route 1, Box 222
Maupin, Oregon 97037
328-6211

Hood River Ranger District .... 13, 14, 15 (part of), 18, 22, 23, 24, 25, 26, 27, 28
6780 Highway 35 South
Mt. Hood-Parkdale, Oregon 97041
666-0701 (Portland)
352-6002 (other)

Barlow Ranger District .... 15 (part of), 16, 17, 19, 20, 21
P.O. Box 67
Dufur, Oregon 97021
467-2291

Estacada Ranger District 32, 33
595 N.W. Industrial Way
Estacada, Oregon 97023
630-6861

Clackamas Ranger District 34
61431 E. Highway 224
Estacada, Oregon 97023
630-4256

INTRODUCTION

If it weren't for all terrain bikes, or mountain bikes as they usually are called, a lot of bicycle shops would not be in business today because, in 1989, those ATBs's accounted for about seventy percent of total unit sales. This guide is for those who have mountain bikes and would like to know where to ride them. Thanks primarily to the logging industry there are thousands of miles of roads through scenic and unfamiliar terrain that aren't suitable for hiking or the family auto (and in many cases, not any four wheeled motorized vehicle) but are perfect for mountain bikes. About one-third of the rides in this guide are along trails for varying proportions of their distances. Riders interested in pursuing more trail riding can refer to the various hiking guide books currently in print. However, note that most of these trails actually aren't suitable for cycling, are located in wilderness areas, in which bicycles are prohibited, or have been specifically closed to bikes. Also, be aware that bicycles are not permitted on the entire Pacific Crest Trail, are prohibited on most of the trails on the Oregon side of the Columbia River Gorge and on many other routes in the Mt. Hood National Forest.

People who have been hard recreational road riders (i.e. a very fast and hilly 80 miles is their idea of a fun romp) and have then tried mountain bikes immediately realize that comparing the two is like comparing apples and oranges. Both styles are indeed bicycles and in the most basic sense are ridden essentially the same way. But beyond that each type has its own particular characteristics. At some time on their very first mountain bike outing, those experienced road riders are going to realize the distance that is enjoyable on an ATB is about one-fourth that on a road bike. No more trying to run down or outrun other cyclists unless they're also on mountain bikes—and then it can be like pedaling in molasses. And no more out sprinting dogs—unless you are exceptionally swift and the dog is extremely infirm. One bonus is that, by now, many dogs don't even bother chasing mountain bikes because it just isn't sporting enough. It also doesn't take too long for an experienced road cyclist to adjust to the fact that, although he would never, ever walk his bike up a steep paved road no matter how much his legs and lungs hurt, he's absolutely going to have to dismount from time to time—unless he just sticks to rides with reasonable grades and surfaces. Of course, the tradeoff is that a mountain bike can take you to all manner of new, fun, scenic and, if you want, challenging, places that a road bike could never reach.

HOW TO USE THIS BOOK

The sequential numbering of the rides in this guide was determined by road access: Numbers 1 and 2 are off I-84 at the western end of the Columbia River Gorge; Numbers 3 through 11 are off U.S. 26; Numbers 12 through 29 are reached from Oregon 35; Numbers and 30 and 31 are off I-84 at the east end of the Columbia River Gorge; and Numbers 32 through 34 are reached from Oregon 224, which heads southeast from Estacada For riders coming from the east these last three also can be reached by taking Forest Service Roads 42 and 58 west from U.S. 26 south of Wapinitia Pass—refer to the Mt. Hood Forest Recreation Map if you intend to take this approach.

CAPSULES

DIFFICULTY This combines the amount and severity of the climbing with the surface and the length, all of which are described in more detail in the next two listings in the Capsule. Mountain bikers quickly learn that, along with distance, it's the combination of grade and surface that determines the difficulty. An extremely steep road with a very firm surface is no big deal and can be ascended very quickly, whereas a levelish one with large, loose rocks is slow going and a test of nerves and reflexes. This is made no easier by knowing that, if it's an in and out trip, you'll be getting no free ride on the way back. Of course, what is easy, moderate and hard is a relative thing to each person. The grading in this guide is geared to the rider who is in reasonably good shape and has normal motor skills. Of course, the authors' idea of what's difficult and yours might not be the same, but they have tried to be

3

consistent, so that after a couple of rides you should know what the rating really means in relation to your own experience.

SURFACE Distances are given for paved roads, unpaved roads and trails. The three are always shown, even if there is no actual mileage for one or two of them. Appropriate descriptive adjectives accompany the unpaved road and trail sections to give you a better idea of what to expect. A few of the rides could have eliminated some of the paved and even unpaved road riding (such as No.'s 20 and 23) but these sections were included because they are enjoyable to cycle, travel through scenic terrain and/or add some distance. Also, they usually provide a fun, free ride back. However, if your inclination is to shorten a ride, you can sometimes determine an optional starting point from reading the cycling log and, in a few cases, referring to the Recreation Map for the Mt. Hood National Forest.

DISTANCE Mileage is given one way if the ride retraces itself on the way back but round trip mileage is shown if the route is a loop. Note that the mileages given in the Surface section also follow this pattern: one way only if the ride is in and out and total mileage if the ride is a loop.

ELEVATION GAIN Altitude gained for a loop includes all the uphill—i.e. if you lose elevation the amount of climbing you do to recoup that loss is shown in the total. However, for one way trips any downhill is shown as an elevation loss and you need to add it to the elevation gain to determine the total amount of climbing on the ride.

HIGH POINT This is an aid in helping you determine if a route might be snow free. Also, discovering you're at a higher elevation than you're used to may make you feel better about any exceptionally heavy breathing.

USUALLY OPEN The precise time the route is open is, of course, dependent on how early the first snows come and how soon the old snows melt. If you have suspicions, refer to the listing elsewhere in this guide that indicates which Ranger District has jurisdiction of which rides and phone the appropriate Ranger Station. As it is with many other outdoor activities, the finer points of the scenery along the bike rides change throughout the times the routes are open—delights such as the wildflowers of midsummer, the huckleberries of August, the turning larch of October. However, when you plan fall rides, pay attention to the opening weeks of hunting season. Most riders will opt to stay out of the woods then.

No supplementary maps have been listed because the Recreation Map for the Mt. Hood National Forest covers all the rides in this guide. They cost from $2 to $4, depending on where they are obtained, and can be purchased at any of the Ranger Stations or the Headquarters of the Mt. Hood National Forest in Gresham at 2955 N.W. Division Street. In downtown Portland, they are also available at the U. S. Forest Service's Information Center, 319 S.W. Pine, and from commercial outlets, such as Powell's Travel Store in Pioneer Square and Captain's Nautical, 138 N.W. 10th Ave., and at most outdoor stores.

The first part of the text is a brief description of the route's special characteristics—if it has exceptionally steep trails, poses particular challenges, presents especially noteworthy scenery, etc. Where relevant, driving directions are given from both the west and east. Note that the Exit numbers on I-84 correspond with the mileage from the Willamette River in downtown Portland. For example, Exit 64 is 64 miles east of that point. For rides that begin east of the junction of U.S. 26 and Oregon 35 you may find your car's odometer is several tenths of a mile in disagreement with distances given in the text because the beginning and end of the interchange there is so ill-defined.

The mileages indicate junctions or other relevant features. When a mileage has been given to a hundredth (i.e. 18.4 followed by 18.45) it means there is less than 0.1 mile difference between two turns. Note that mileages are not given at the junctions of some side roads when the correct route is entirely obvious and unambiguous, although those routes may be shown on the ride maps. Road numbers listed in the logs may not always appear on signs in the field. They have been included to help you in identifying your position on the maps. Mileages in the body of the log match noteworthy features and will also help you stay oriented with the map. Since every one's bicycle computer odometer probably registers a bit differently, your mileage may vary slightly from the log. However, assuming both the odometer used for this guide and yours are consistent, you'll be able to determine the precise difference on the first ride and apply it to future ones. The authors have made a deliberate decision that the primary purpose of the copy is to get you to the start of the ride and keep you on the route. Once that is taken care of, space limitations unfortunately usually preclude including anything more than cursory comments on the physical and cultural aspects of the trip. Left out are such tidbits as the wispy larch trees that turn a luminescent yellow around late October and appear on portions of rides such as No's. 18, 19 and 20, or the conies you are certain to hear and see at the 11.2 mile point of ride No 14. However, the authors usually have managed to find space to note particularly dense patches of huckleberry bushes, the fruit of which normally ripens by the second half of August.

Unlike hiking trails, which are reasonably stable in their alignment and condition, mountain bike routes tend to be much more subject to change. Although all the routes in this guide were ridden by the authors in the summer and fall of 1989, logging and road building, etc. between then and now could have changed some of them. Rides that follow trails are also subject to the forces of Nature, particularly from blowdown. Or, a road that once had a good surface might since have been spread with big, loose gravel. And these changes can work the other way, too—a road that was originally unpaved, bumpy and fun could be graded or, even worse, paved! The wise mountain biker accepts all the above and the prudent one always has an alternate ride to take in case the first choice has so drastically changed that it just doesn't go. This shouldn't be too much of a problem because usually there are good options nearby. Also, people who do a lot of mountain biking quickly develop a flexible mind set. Speaking of logging, if you do a few of these rides on weekdays you may encounter loaded log trucks on the road and even find yourself passing a logging operation. Usually, you can hear both long before you meet them. However, if you want to avoid one or the other entirely, you can phone the appropriate Ranger Station and inquire if logging activity is currently in progress.

Selection of various types of mountain bicycles, their maintenance, types of cycling clothing, riding techniques, etc. are covered extensively in many books and magazine articles and will not be dealt with here, except for a listing of safety and mechanical items you should carry with you on all rides.

A minimum of two full water bottles. Even on the shortest of rides an injured cyclist, although he or she may be quite near a good access road, might have to wait a long time to be rescued. Dehydration can be very insidious when cycling and common wisdom dictates that the rider must drink before becoming thirsty. Also, mountain cycling does not usually provide enough wind blast to cool the body efficiently. The rider compensates by sweating more profusely per mile than he or she does when road cycling.

First Aid Kit.

Space Blanket. Even in mild weather conditions an injured cyclist may go into shock and need extra body radiation entrapment. In a high wind a cyclist can get very cold just sitting down to have lunch. Always carry gloves and ear warmers and also leg warmers, if you're riding in the mountains with short pants.

Flashlight. Just because you don't plan to be out after dark doesn't mean it can't happen.

Also carry the remaining items, but remember they won't actually do you any good unless you know how to use them:

Compass and a Mt. Hood National Forest Recreation Map. Sooner or later, you'll want to do some exploring beyond the boundaries of the maps that accompany each ride and the rec map will show the options. And then there could be those times when you're inadvertently on an unplanned route...

Tool Kit. This should include wrenches for all nuts and allen head screws found on your bike.

Chain Rivet Tool. If a derailleur should break in the middle of nowhere the chain can be destaked and shortened to accommodate the lowest gear needed for the return trip, thus bypassing the broken rear shifter. Also, a damaged link can be removed and replaced in the field.

Spoke Wrench and Extra Spokes. In the case of a broken spoke you have three choices: Either open up the brake calipers so that the wobbly wheel will not rub on the break pads, retrue the wheel or replace the broken spoke. Most of the time spokes break off on the freewheel side of the rear hub and, unless you have high flange hubs and drilled out gears, replacing a spoke in the field will be virtually impossible as it takes a huge amount of torque to remove the freewheel body—even with the proper remover and pipe wrench (not to mention a long pipe on the end of the wrench to provide still more torque).

Extra Foldable Tire, Extra Tube and a Tire Patch Kit. Aggressive mountain tires may seem invulnerable but a large side cut can instantly render them useless. It's also a good idea to carry a strip of canvas or similar material to temporarily patch the inside of a tire that has a very large puncture tear in the casing.

Tire Pump. Be sure to have a mountain style fat tire pump because a regular road pump puts out much less air volume. You want to spend your time and energy on the bike, not next to it.

As with life in general, there are rules of conduct for mountain bikers (and those who don't follow this etiquette cause distress for themselves and others). Most importantly: *Do not ride where you're not supposed to*. This means stay off all private land, stay out of Wilderness Areas, the entire Pacific Crest Trail and any route that is signed as closed to bicycles. When you are on a legal route and you encounter hikers or horsemen, give them the right-of-way (be especially courteous to the latter).

If you're interested in riding with groups, visit a store that sells mountain bikes and the staff there or the bulletin board will supply the information.

Good Biking!

D.L.
R.L.

Waucoma Ridge

AREA MAP

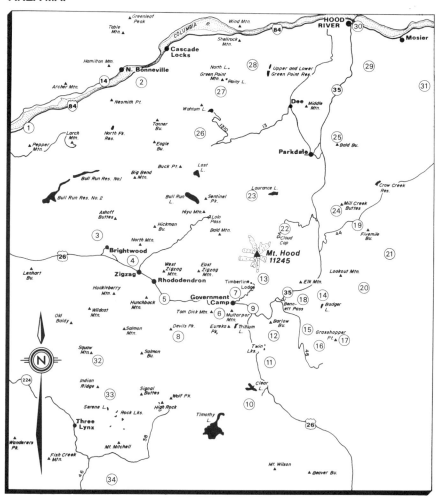

CONTENTS

LEGEND

☆	Start of Ride
➤	Ride Direction
▬	Paved Road
═	Gravel Road
====	Dirt Road
----	Trail
•••••••	Cross Country Route
No. 415	Trail No.
137	Road No.
△	Campground
2.8	Mileage

1 PALMER MILL ROAD LOOP

Difficulty: Moderate (except for initial steep 1.3 miles)
Surface: 10 miles on paved roads; 10 miles on mostly smooth unpaved roads; 0 mile on trails
Distance: 20 miles round trip
Elevation gain: 2,700 feet round trip
High point: 2,570 feet
Usually open May through November

The lower end of Palmer Mill Road begins from the Columbia River Scenic Highway above the community of Bridal Veil, climbs through a variety of wooded terrain to Larch Mountain Road and then after six miles of fun paved downhill turns onto a connector to Palmer Mill Road. If there's a strong wind through the Gorge its affect will be noticed for only the first and last 0.1 mile of the circuit. Although following the loop described below is recommended because it goes through less familiar terrain, cyclists who want a longer ride can continue west along Larch Mountain Road to its junction with the Scenic Highway and follow the latter back past Crown Point and Latourell Falls to the starting point.

Drive east from Portland on I-84 to the Bridal Veil Exit 28 (not accessible to west bound traffic), follow the exit road up for 0.2 mile to the junction with the Scenic Highway and park in the area between the two roads. If you're approaching from the east, take the Ainsworth Park Exit 35 and continue west on the Scenic Highway for 7.1 miles. If you're coming from the west along the Scenic Highway, drive 5.3 miles east of Crown Point.

00.0 ..Head west along the Scenic Highway.

00.1 ..Turn left onto Palmer Mill Road. You'll most likely have to walk along some sections—just keep in mind that it's a small percentage of the whole ride. A couple of tenths mile beyond a side stream at 1.4 miles the grade becomes more moderate and continues so for the remainder of the ride.

01.9 ..Stay left at the unsigned junction of Brower Road. If you make the recommended loop, you'll be returning along the route on your right. Up to this point you've been traversing high on the east wall of Bridal Veil Creek canyon, but beyond the fork you'll be following beside, or close to, the stream for about 4.0 miles. Stay straight on the main road at several side roads.

05.6 ..Stay right on the main road. (If you want to do some exploring on the rough road toward Multnomah Basin you could turn left here and then right after 0.2 mile.)

07.5 ..Turn right onto paved Larch Mountain Road (Forest Road 15) and begin descending.

13.4 ..Turn right onto paved Brower Road. You'll have a few short uphills along this final paved section. At 15.2 miles pass an unpaved spur on the right that heads northeast for 1.0 mile to the site of the former fire lookout on Pepper Mountain.

15.4 ..Stay straight (right) on Brower Road at the junction of paved Haines Road, which connects with the Larch Mountain Road, and in 2.0 miles come to the end of the pavement.

18.1 ..Turn left at the junction of Palmer Mill Road, the route you followed in.

19.9 ..Turn right onto the Scenic Highway.

20.0 ..End of ride.

Taking a break after a steep climb

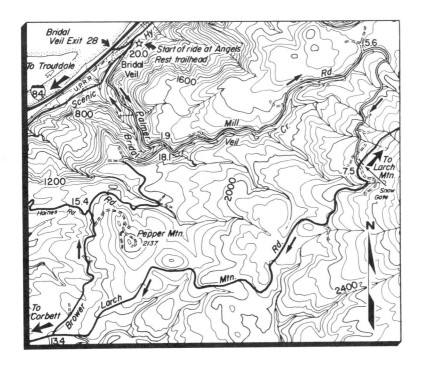

2   TANNER CREEK ROAD

Difficulty: Moderate
Surface: **0 mile on paved roads; 5.9 miles on unpaved roads that are occasionally rough, but never a problem to ride; 0 mile on trails**
Distance: 5.9 miles one way
Elevation gain: 1,600 feet; loss 500 feet
High point: 1,680 feet
Usually open March through November

This fun road ride that begins from the Bonneville Dam interchange off I-84 is an outing for all seasons: It's the second lowest elevation trip in this guide (No. 30 is the lowest), so it affords about the first chance to enjoy the greenery and flowers of spring; in summer the lush canopy of trees offers welcome shade; in fall all the maples have turned color; and in late fall and early spring that same low elevation usually provides a snow-free, if somewhat austere, setting. All this vegetation does not preclude several good views, both down onto Bonneville Dam, to other points in the Columbia River Gorge and even into the Bull Run Reserve. Note that the road is shaded in winter, so once it's ice- or snow-covered, it can take a long time to melt. Although not heavily used, the route is open to private vehicles for the first 3.1 miles. Also note that trees may be down over the southern sections of the ride. However, because many have fallen from the high side of the road you'll be able to go under most of them.

Drive on I-84 to the Bonneville Dam Exit 40. If you've come from the west, turn right at the end of the exit and immediately come to a T-junction, if you've come from the east, turn left and go through the tunnel under the freeway. You can turn right at the fork and drive several hundred feet to the large parking area for the Tanner Falls Trail or, if you're wary of car clouting, you can leave your vehicle off to the side at the T-junction or in the Bonneville Dam Fish Hatchery parking lot.

00.0 .. Cycle to the east up the unpaved road from the T-junction just south of the exit, following the sign to Tanner Butte and Tanner Creek Trails. Although the grade is erratic and never steep, you will be climbing for the next 4.0 miles.

00.3 .. Turn right at a fork in front of a large water tank and pass a sign identifying the road as No. 777. At 0.7 mile have a view down onto Bonneville Dam and the new ship lock. At 1.0 mile the grade moderates and the surface becomes smoother (this first portion is the roughest of the ride). Curve right at 1.2 miles.

01.4 .. Stay left (straight) on the main road. Several spurs veer off from Tanner Creek Road, but you'll have no trouble figuring out the main route. Curious riders with extra energy could explore some of these power line tower access roads. At 2.5 miles pass the start of the Tanner Butte Trail, which is explicitly closed to bicycles.

03.1 .. Come to a gate, go around or under it and continue uphill—very soon at a more moderate angle—to a viewpoint at 4.0 miles where you'll probably want to stop and look around. Munra Point is the highest grassy nubbin on the long, narrow ridge to the northwest. The solitary peak to the southwest is Mt. Talapus in the Bull Run Reserve. Farther on you'll pass two more viewpoints similar to this one. Begin descending and continue gradually downhill for the remainder of the ride to the turnaround point. Despite what you might dread, the climb back is easy. At 5.8 miles pass the start of the Tanner Creek Trail, which is closed to bicycles because it almost immediately enters the Columbia Wilderness. Continue down the road and begin dropping very steeply for less than 0.1 mile.

05.9 .. Come to the end of the road at the base of a power line tower. If you want to stop for a snack, walk 75 yards along an overgrown bed to the bank of a small creek. The old road continues to Tanner Creek, but it's very bushy.

Munra Point from Tanner Creek Road

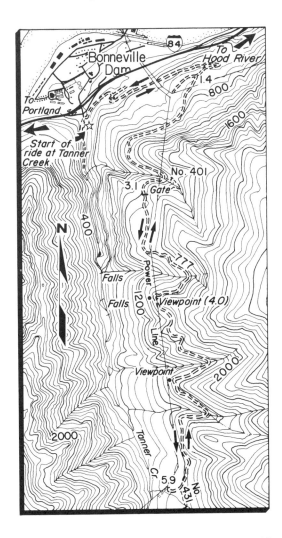

3 MARMOT LOOP

Difficulty: Moderate
Surface: 12.7 miles on paved roads; 8.3
miles on mostly good gravel or
dirt roads; 0 mile on trails
Distance: 21 miles round trip
Elevation gain: 2,700 feet
High point: 2,300 feet
Usually open March through December

Because of good surfaces and reasonable grades, the Marmot loop is a perfect introductory trip for cyclists who are in shape, but new to mountain biking. Both they and experienced riders will be delighted by the scenery, which includes views of Mt. Hood, the southern edge of the Bull Run Reserve, Little Sandy River Canyon and the grassy expanse of a 1,000 acre cattle ranch.

Take U.S. 26 for 12 miles east of Sandy and turn north on the road to Brightwood. This junction is 0.8 mile east of the 36 mile post. After 0.6 mile turn left onto East Brightwood Bridge Road at a store and tavern, in 0.2 mile come to a large open area on the left just before a bridge and park here. If you're approaching from the east, you can take the easterly end of East Brightwood Loop Road from U.S. 26 for about two miles to the junction at the store and tavern.

00.0 .. Cycle north across the bridge over the Sandy River.

00.1 .. Turn left on East Barlow Trail Road. On weekdays you'll be sharing the road with trucks for 0.3 mile until their turnoff to a gravel operation. Riders who do the Crutcher Bench circuit (No. 4) will be coming out on that access road.

00.9 .. Turn right onto paved Forest Road 14 and, except for one short respite, begin a 4.0 mile climb. If you are doing the ride on a weekday you'll probably meet several log trucks. However, Road 14 is a wide two lanes, complete with yellow center line, and you can hear the trucks coming well ahead of their appearances. Soon enter a clearcut and continue up in the open until you re-enter mostly alder woods at 2.7 miles. Have that one short level and downhill section around 3.2 miles.

04.9 .. Stay left on the unpaved road heading downhill at a shallow angle. Just ahead on the paved route is a sign stating that Road 14 is closed by a gate 300 feet ahead. Descend along the unpaved road, which is identified as 2503, the route you'll be following for the next 9.2 miles until you intersect Marmot Road. After 1.4 miles of downhill begin an easy climb and at 6.8 miles come to a viewpoint where you can see Mt. Hood, directly down onto a double falls on the Little Sandy River and across the valley into the Bull Run Reserve. The flat-topped peak with the lookout to the left (northwest) of Mt. Hood is Hickman Butte. Resume descending and travel on an uncharacteristically rough section.

07.2 .. Curve left—do not take spur 115, which ends in 0.3 mile—and continue downhill.

07.9 .. Stay straight (right) at a fork.

08.0 .. Stay straight and farther on begin descending along a valley wall.

08.7 .. Turn very sharply right, after several yards pass a sign indicating you're still on Road 2503 and in 0.3 mile begin climbing.

09.5 .. Stay straight (left) on the main road. Continue climbing out of the little valley you entered near 8.0 miles and eventually curve right.

09.9 .. Stay straight on the main road, travel at an increasingly gradual grade for 0.2 mile and then begin a fun 3.0 mile downhill stretch.

13.2 .. Stay left at a fork where the pavement resumes and in 0.4 mile begin climbing steeply (the last noteworthy uphill on the ride).

14.1 .. Turn left onto Marmot Road, resume descending and after 1.5 miles come to that promised cattle ranch.

19.2 .. Turn left onto East Barlow Trail Road. The section to the right goes to U.S. 26.

21.0 .. Turn right onto East Brightwood Bridge Road and cross the river to your starting point.

Mt. Hood and Little Sandy River Canyon

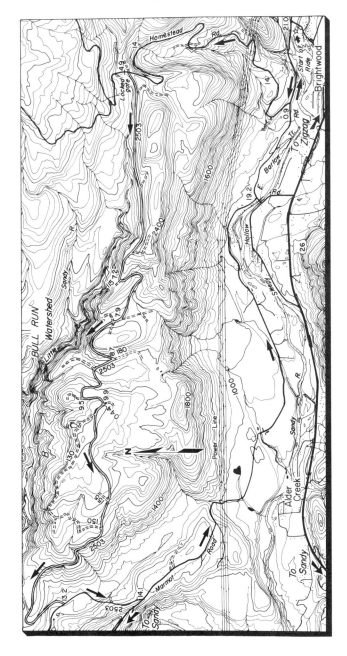

4 CRUTCHER BENCH LOOP

Difficulty: Hard because of sections of steep uphill and some rough stretches
Surface: 10.1 miles on paved roads; 6.6 miles on unpaved roads with about half the distance on reasonably good surfaces and the other half rocky and/or rough; 0 mile on trails
Distance: 16.7 miles round trip
Elevation gain: 1,250 feet
High point: 2,300 feet
Usually open late March through November

Crutcher Bench is on the ridge that parallels the north side of U.S. 26 just west of the community of Zigzag. The route follows a B.P.A. power line access road for the middle third of the loop, affording unobstructed sightings back to nearby Mt. Hood early on and then views down over the Sandy River Valley and across to a portion of the Salmon-Huckleberry Wilderness.

Note that the farthest west part of this loop follows a road through a private gravel quarry. As of 1989 this road continued to be open to public travel, with the proviso that visitors follow it at their own risk. So, hold the thought that this status might change.

Drive on U.S. 26 for 17 miles east of the east end of Sandy or 2.0 miles west of Rhododendron to the community of Zigzag (0.3 mile east of the 42 mile post), turn south into the entrance to the Zigzag Ranger Station and leave your car at the far (east) end of the parking area.

00.0 .. From the entrance to the Ranger Station head west on U.S. 26.

00.1 .. Turn right (north) on East Lolo Pass Road.

01.3 .. Stay straight (right) on East Lolo Pass Road at the junction of East Barlow Trail Road to your left, along which you'll be returning.

02.8 .. Turn left onto unpaved East Carnarvon Road. Initially head north and then curve southwest (left) as you come near the power line cut.

03.3 .. Stay straight (left) where East Anglesley Road heads right. Two-tenths mile farther come to a bridge and soon begin a 1.1 mile long, very steep climb.

04.7 .. Stay straight (left) a short distance after the road levels off and where a spur heads right. You're now on the north end of Crutcher Bench, named for a man who filed a homestead claim in the area in the 1890's.

05.2 .. Stay straight again where a spur heads left and after about 0.1 mile resume climbing, but at a more reasonable grade. Look back for those views of Mt. Hood. At 5.9 miles the road comes to a crest and gradually begins heading in a northwesterly, rather than a southwesterly, direction. Pass over a large stream at 6.9 miles and a smaller one 0.1 mile farther as you continue to traverse along the power line.

07.5 .. Follow the road that curves down to the left for only about 75 feet and then veer right and follow a less obvious route that takes you right back to the power line. The road that continues downhill comes to unequivocally signed private property before connecting with East Barlow Trail Road. About 75 feet beyond where you rejoin the power line come to a fork. These branches merge in about 0.1 mile. The left is rougher, but better in wet weather because the route to the right can be muddy then. Go by a little stream at 7.7 miles and immediately begin a 0.5 mile climb. By the point you pass an open gate halfway along the ascent you'll have veered to the north away from the power line and entered woods. Have a bit of downhill and then climb at an easier grade.

08.7 .. Stay left (downhill) at a fork at a crest. That's it for the climbing on this loop. Have excellent views to the south as you traverse an open portion of the slope.

09.4 .. Come to a paved road and turn left, continuing downhill. If the quarry is in operation, watch out for dump trucks.

10.2 .. Turn left onto East Barlow Trail Road.

10.5 .. Stay straight (left) and continue east.

15.4 .. Turn right onto East Lolo Pass Road.

16.6 .. Turn left onto U.S. 26.

16.7 .. Turn right to the Zigzag Ranger Station.

Power line access road

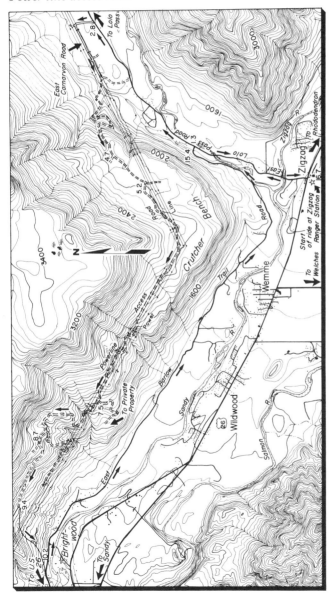

5 PIONEER BRIDLE TRAIL—STILL CREEK ROAD LOOP

Difficulty: Moderate
Surface: 5.6 miles on paved roads; 11.1 miles on good unpaved roads; 9.1 miles on trails and narrow old road beds with only a few short rough or rocky stretches
Distance: 25.8 miles round trip
Elevation gain: 2,550 feet round trip
High point: 3,980 feet
Usually open late May through October

This scenic loop takes the Pioneer Bridle Trail, a combination of narrow old road-beds and wide trails, up to Government Camp. The circuit returns down unpaved Still Creek Road on the other (south) side of Tom Dick and Flag Mountains, which parallel U.S. 26 between Rhododendron and Government Camp.

Drive on U.S. 26 for 0.7 mile east of Rhododendron to the parking area off the south side of the highway identified by a sign stating Route of the Oregon Trail. This is 0.2 mile east of the entrance to Toll Gate Campground and just east of the 45 mile post.

00.0 .. Cycle east through a gate on the Pioneer Bridle Trail No. 795. You'll be meeting several side roads over the next 0.3 mile. Stay straight (left) each time. Beyond this initial section, the route is straightforward. Cross a three-pronged road at 0.4 mile. Where you come to several more north-south roads over the next 2.9 miles, also cross them and continue east.
00.8 .. Turn right onto U.S. 26.
01.0 .. Veer right at the east end of the pedestrian span over the Zigzag River onto the resumption of the Pioneer Bridle Trail.
02.2 .. Stay left—don't follow the road under the power lines. At 3.4 miles abruptly begin climbing on a narrow trail, but in 0.2 mile you'll be back on a wider, more moderately graded tread.
03.9 .. Turn right onto an unpaved road.

03.95 Turn left onto a trail after 50 feet.
04.0 .. Cross U.S. 26 and look for a small sign on a tree that marks the resumption of the trail. Travel on the level for 0.3 mile and then begin climbing along a wide path. Between 4.4 and 4.8 miles make four switchbacks. Because of the rocky tread, you may have to walk portions of these switchbacks. Have a downhill stretch between 5.3 and 5.9 miles, traverse the base of a talus slope and pass a mine shaft on your left at 6.2 miles.
06.4 .. Stay left. The trail to the right goes directly to U.S. 26. Ride mostly downhill for the next 0.3 mile until you go through the pedestrian tunnel under the original Mt. Hood Highway at 6.7 miles.
06.8 .. Turn right onto an unpaved road just above a section of the old highway. For the next mile pass robust huckleberry bushes.
07.1 .. Stay right at fork and continue to parallel U.S. 26 (don't follow the power line cut to the left).
07.5 .. Stay left at a signed X-C ski trail.
08.0 .. Stay right at the X-C ski trail to Enid Lake.
08.3 .. Stay straight at a connector to Glacier View Road you've been paralleling for the last 0.1 mile. If you prefer, you can take this paved road to U.S. 26. Whichever, just Do Not turn left.
08.6 .. Turn left (east) on U.S. 26.
08.9 .. For a food stop, turn left onto the Government Camp business loop, which rejoins U.S. 26 at a State rest area. Or, you can continue east on U.S. 26.
10.5 .. Stay straight on U.S. 26 at the junction of Timberline Road.
10.8 .. Turn right onto Road 2650 to Still Creek Campground and head downhill through the camp area. Come to the end of the pavement at 11.6 miles.
12.0 .. Turn right onto Road 126.
12.5 .. Turn right onto Road 2612, Still Creek Road, and begin 12.8 miles of almost all downhill. Initially, the gravel surface is a bit loose, but it's no problem and the road is increasingly better as you head west.
13.7 .. Stay straight (left) on the main road. Cross bridges over Still Creek at 17.2, 18.2, 19.0 and 20.6 miles. At 22.7 miles resume traveling on pavement.
24.2 .. Turn right onto Road 20.
25.3 .. Turn right onto the trail that parallels U.S. 26 through the campground.
25.8 .. End of ride.

Sign at start of ride

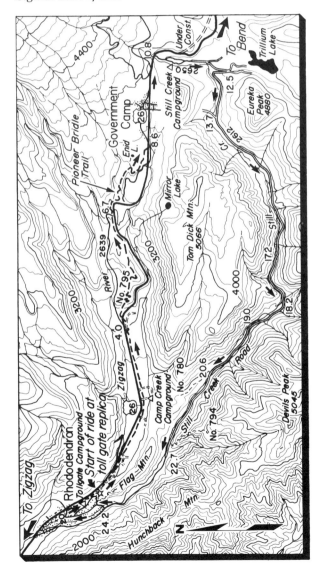

6 WIND LAKE

Difficulty: Moderately hard because of some steep sections
Surface: 0 mile on paved roads; 3.4 miles on occasionally rough and/or steep unpaved roads; 0 mile on trails
Distance: 3.4 miles one way
Elevation gain: 1,190 feet; loss 390 feet
High point: 5,027 feet
Usually open July through October

Wind Lake perches on the south slope of Tom Dick Mountain—the ridge whose north side supports the Multorpor and Ski Bowl ski areas. This ride begins at the first and then zigzags up through the second to the crest of Tom Dick Mountain where it follows an abandoned old roadbed, which is more like a trail, down to the patio of rocks just above the lake's north shore. Later in the summer Wind Lake is warm enough to provide good swimming.

You are encouraged to follow a service spur road for another 0.3 mile along the crest to the upper terminus of the Ski Bowl's highest lift. From here, and also frequently along the ride, you'll have close-up looks at nearby Mt. Hood and south to Mt. Jefferson.

Take U.S. 26 to the business loop through Government Camp and in the middle of town turn south, as indicated by the sign pointing to Multorpor, and drive 0.3 mile to the end of the road. A go cart track may be operating here, but it does not block access.

00.0 .. Ride between the go cart track and the southeast corner of the large blue building and curve right. After a couple of hundred feet continue straight (west)—don't take the road that heads left up to the lodge. The word Multorpor originally was created by the Multorpor Republican Club by combining the first letters of Multnomah, Oregon and Portland.

00.4 .. Stay left after going under a lift and begin climbing. After 0.7 mile pass under the lower chairlift of the Ski Bowl and soon enter a wide cleared swath. Curve left, pass a cabin at 1.5 miles at about the midway point of the open slope and continue up in two turns. At 1.8 miles pass the top of the lift you went under near the beginning of the ride and 0.3 mile farther begin traversing the south, instead of the north, side of the ridge.

02.8 .. Veer left onto a faint old road. This turn is near a light pole 0.1 mile above where you come near the crest of the ridge at a saddle and 0.7 mile beyond where you crossed to the south side of the ridge. After a smooth stretch the surface is rough and eroded but then is grassy before coming to just above the lake.

03.4 .. Wind Lake
To make the recommended 0.3 mile side trip to the top of the lift, continue along the main road from the turnoff to Wind Lake at 2.8 miles. The bed is extremely rough for several hundred feet but then improves. After 0.2 mile curve right and head east to the top of the chair. You'll have a bird's-eye view over the runs of the Ski Bowl (the steepest in the Mt. Hood area), down onto Government Camp and across to features on the south side of Mt. Hood such as Timberline Lodge and the routes of the Glade and Alpine Trails (No. 7).

Ski Bowl and Mt. Hood

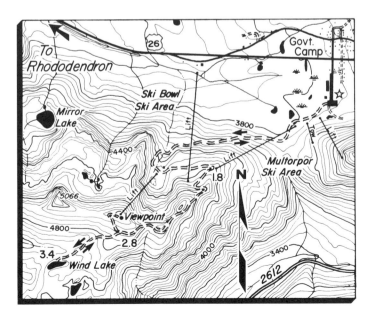

7 ALPINE—GLADE SKI TRAILS LOOP

Difficulty: Very difficult because of sections of steep, rough treads
Surface: 1 mile on paved roads; 1 mile on dirt roads; 5 miles on trails
Distance: 7 miles round trip
Elevation gain: 2,100 feet
High point: 5,960 feet
Usually open mid July through early October

Because of their often steep grades and rough surfaces, the Alpine and Glade Ski Trails, which connect Government Camp and Timberline Lodge, provide the most technically demanding riding in this guide. However, the less intrepid who don't mind walking their bikes more than usual will also enjoy the loop, particularly the lower 1.5 miles of the Glade Trail, which affords easy, fun riding. If you plan to make the entire loop, it's recommended you follow the Alpine Trail up, because of its firmer surface and ill-defined alignment at the top. A considerably easier option for those who don't enjoy—or can't manage—steep uphill grades is to climb along paved West Leg Road, which would add about 2.0 miles, and then descend on the Glade or Alpine Trails.

If you intend to follow the Alpine Trail down, instead of the itinerary described below, and aren't familiar with the area, you should pick the Alpine Trail up at the 2.5 mile point of the log. To reach this point from Timberline Lodge, cycle downhill (as if you were heading to U.S. 26) to just below where a one way loop to the huge parking lot begins, turn right onto the upper end of West Leg Road and follow it 0.6 mile.

Drive on U.S. 26 to the east end of the Government Camp business loop to Summit Ski Area. It shares a parking lot with a State rest area just to the east.

00.0 ..Begin from the northwest side of the parking lot, go around a couple of small buildings and follow the service road up the ski area. At 0.3 mile stay on the road as it curves right and 0.3 mile farther come to the top of the cleared slope.

01.0 ..Stay straight where you pass just yards from West Leg Road. (If you're planning on taking the road the rest of the way up, bail out here.) One tenth mile farther come to the bottom of Big Mazama Hill, the steepest portion of the Alpine Trail. You'll most likely be walking for the next 0.4 mile. But you'll be entertained by views south to Mt. Jefferson, Trillium Lake and the Multorpor Ski Area (see No. 6) and north to nearby Mt. Hood.

For those who are interested in food for the stomach as well as the eyes, wild strawberries line much of the route and huckleberry bushes are especially dense just beyond the top of Big Mazama Hill.

02.3 ..Come to the bottom of the Blossom Chairlift. Go around the west side of the lower terminus and then follow a road east (do not head up the run).

02.5 ..Turn left onto West Leg Road.

02.7 ..Veer left off the road onto a faint path traversing a grassy slope. (Don't fret if you miss this—just continue along West Leg Road for 0.4 mile to where it meets Timberline Road, turn left, stay right almost immediately at the lower end of the loop road and pedal uphill for 0.6 mile to the top of the immense parking area. Head west, passing the Day Lodge and Timberline Lodge, for 0.2 mile to the top of Alpine Trail.) After you enter woods bear right (east), come to a service road along a lighted run at 3.0 mile and follow it up to the west side of Timberline Lodge.

03.2 ..Turn left (west) onto the paved road.

03.3 ..Stay left and begin descending along the wide, signed Glade Trail, the route of an aerial tramway in the 1950's.

04.6 ..Veer right off the service road onto a fainter route. A tall, orange Glade Trail sign off the left side of the road points right to this route. This is an important junction, so be watching for it. It's easy going from now on. At 6.1 miles begin traveling on a service road, 0.1 mile farther come to an oiled road and follow it past homes.

06.4 ..Stay left on an unpaved road.

06.5 ..Turn left onto the business loop through Government Camp.

07.0 ..End of ride at Summit Ski Area.

Timberline Lodge

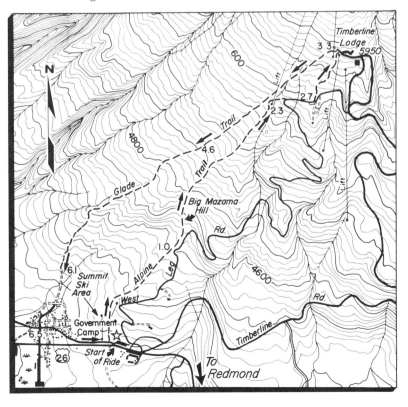

8 KINZEL LAKE

Difficulty: Moderate
Surface: 0.8 mile on paved roads; 10.6
miles on unpaved, occasionally
rough roads; 0 mile on trails
Distance: 11.4 miles one way
Elevation gain: 1,640 feet; loss 1,160 feet
High point: 4,750 feet
Usually open July through October

The route to Kinzel Lake follows the Sherar Burn Road along the south wall of the immense valley of the Salmon River. Although this sometimes rough road is open to vehicles, it's not heavily traveled.

Take U.S. 26 for 0.3 mile east of the road to Timberline Lodge just beyond the east end of Government Camp to a wide turnoff on the south side of the road and park here. Later in the season the large sign that identifies this as the entrance to Still Creek Campground may not be up.

00.0 .. Ride down through the campground. The pavement ends after 0.8 mile.

01.1 .. Turn right onto Road 126. The route that continues straight meets the paved road to Trillium Lake.

01.7 .. Stay straight on Road 2613 at a four-way junction. The road to the left also goes to Trillium Lake and the one to the right descends along the valley holding Still Creek (No. 5). The next 8.6 miles of mostly uphill are interrupted by several short level or downhill stretches. As often happens, on the return trip you'll probably feel that there's a lot more climbing than there was descending going in. With snow cover, this road is a popular cross-country ski route. Have views south to Mt. Jefferson and Olallie Butte. On the ride back you'll have many sightings of a considerably closer Mt. Hood. And if you look at just the right time, you'll see Mt. Adams.

Come to Eureka Saddle at 3.4 miles and at 5.6 miles pass the start of the Veda Lake Trail on the right and on the left the Fir Tree Trail, which in a short distance enters the Salmon-Huckleberry Wilderness. At 7.6 miles round a corner and have views ahead to the rugged crest of the ridge. At 10.3 miles begin the final descent. Along one section you can see ahead to the fire lookout on the summit of Devils Peak.

10.9 .. Turn left. (The route that continues straight ends in 0.4 mile.) Descend steeply for 0.4 mile to the small campground and continue along the now level road for 0.1 to near the edge of the lake.

11.4 .. Kinzel Lake

Kinzel Lake

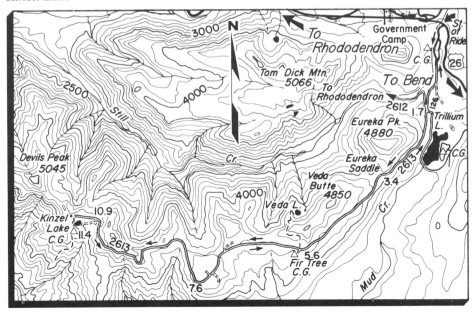

9 WEST FORK FALLS LOOP

Difficulty: Moderately easy
Surface: 0 mile on paved roads; 2.6 miles along good unpaved roads; 2.2 miles along good trails
Distance: 4.8 miles round trip (with several possible side trips)
Elevation gain: 800 feet round trip
High point: 4,600 feet
Usually open late June through October

Cyclists have several options along this loop to a charming, obscure little waterfall between the West Leg and Timberline Roads. The circuit just to the cascades is a good introduction to trail riding. The final 0.6 mile to the falls is steep enough that some beginners may have to walk portions, but they should have no problem riding down. Cyclists wanting a longer outing can explore several side roads and those who enjoy trail riding can continue on a good tread for about 1.3 miles beyond the falls and then retrace their route or return along paved West Leg Road that passes the west end of the unpaved connector crossed at 1.9 miles.

Drive on U.S. 26 for 1.4 miles east of the junction of Timberline Road, which is just east of Government Camp, to Snow Bunny Lodge off the north side of the highway and park here.

00.0 .. Take the unpaved road that begins from the northwest corner of the Lodge parking area.

00.1 .. Turn left on Road 228 and climb at a mostly moderate grade. You'll be returning along the road (No. 226) that continues straight here.

00.9 .. Turn right onto the trail identified by blue diamond markers and a sign stating Yellow Jacket Trail, a cross-country ski route that traverses between Timberline Road and White River Canyon. Note that the one section you'll be following originally was a hiking trail and that's why it has such a good tread.

01.3 .. Veer left, continuing on the good trail.

01.4 .. Stay left on the trail where blue diamonds indicate the Yellow Jacket Trail

heads up to the right. You might not even note this junction because the route of the cross-country ski trail is so rough. Cross a perpendicular tread after 0.1 mile.

01.6 .. Meet the Timberline Road and cross it, angling about 75 feet up to the right. Look for blazes and drop to the resumption of the trail.

01.9 .. Come to a connector between West Leg Road and its predecessor, the East Leg Road, cross it and resume traveling on a trail. After visiting the falls, you'll be taking the section of this connector to the southeast. The part that heads west meets the West Leg Road after 0.7 mile at a point 1.7 miles above U.S. 26. Climb in woods and then a clearing, re-enter woods and level off several hundred feet before coming to the view of the falls.

02.5 .. If you don't intend to make the extension, turn around at the stream above the waterfall. (If you want to do more trail riding on the trail, which was cleared of many downed trees in 1990, cross the stream and traverse along the east side of the flow. Pass the main stream coming in on your left, cross to the other side of the little canyon and recross to the east side several hundred yards farther.

About 200 feet beyond where you go back to the west side be watching for a switchback on your left at a downed log and take it. Eventually, cross the old Blossom Ski Trail, switch back and recross it, veering very slightly left. Cross the trail a final time and in a couple of hundred feet come to a dirt road. The pavement of West Leg Road to the left is hard to spot, but you'll have no trouble seeing cars that might be on it. Follow the road about 2.5 miles down to its junction with the unpaved connector.)

03.1 .. Return to the connector between the East Leg and West Leg Roads, turn left (east) and ride on the level.

03.3 .. Come to the Timberline Road and cross it to the obvious resumption of the road. The ride is mostly easy downhill for the rest of the loop.

03.5 .. Stay straight (left). The road to the right is one you can explore if you want a longer ride.

03.8 .. Stay straight (right) where a road comes in on the left.

04.7 .. Stay straight (left) at the junction of the road you took in.

04.8 .. Come to your starting point.

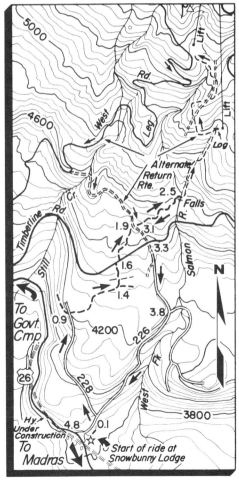

The map shows a trail route with the following markings:

5000
4600
4200
3800

Rd.
West Leg
Alternate Return Rte.
2.5
Falls
1.9
3.1
3.3
1.6
3.8
1.4
0.9
226
228
4.8
0.1

Lift
Lift
Log

Cr.

Timberline Rd
Still

Salmon R.
West Fk.

N

26

To Govt. Cmp

Hy. Under Construction
To Madras

Start of ride at Snowbunny Lodge

10 CLEAR LAKE BUTTE LOOP

Difficulty: Moderately hard because of 0.7 mile of steep and rough sections of trail
Surface: 11.1 miles on paved roads; 8.9 miles on good unpaved roads; 4.1 miles on trails
Distance: 24.1 miles round trip
Elevation gain: 2,520 feet round trip
High point: 4,454 feet
Usually open late June through October

Instead of having to take paved roads most of the way to the fire lookout on Clear Lake Butte, which along with the one on Flag Point (No. 20) is among the few remaining staffed towers anywhere, mountain bikers have the option of reaching it by a considerably more challenging and interesting route that includes a stretch of seldom used trail and a shoreline circuit around most of Clear Lake.

From the junction of U.S. 26 and Oregon 35, which is 2.6 miles east of Government Camp, drive south on U.S. 26 for 6.7 miles and turn left into the signed Frog Lake Campground and Sno-Park. Outhouses are located at the northeast side.

00.0 .. Turn right (north) onto U.S. 26.
00.05 Cross U.S. 26 to the possibly unsigned Pacific Crest Trail that heads west.
00.1 .. Turn left onto signed Trail 483. The Pacific Crest Trail continues straight (west) and is closed to bicycles. Very soon begin 0.6 mile of steep, rough tread, up which all but the exceptional few will have to push their bikes. This pitch, one section along the edge of a clearcut and a short, rocky stretch are the only parts most people should have to walk. Cross a narrow, gravel road at 0.9 mile.

01.7 .. Come to a 1989 clearcut, go around the left side and then veer right and intersect the trail at 1.8 miles. Begin descending at 2.3 miles and in the middle of that rocky stretch at 3.2 miles have views of Mt. Jefferson and your destination.
03.7 .. Cross a road and continue downhill on No. 483 along the best trail surface of the ride.
04.1 .. Turn right onto very good, oiled Road 2630.
05.3 .. Turn left onto an unpaved road. This is a short distance beyond where the oiled road crosses a creek and curves to the left. Soon begin traveling along the shore of Clear Lake on an enjoyably bumpy bed. You may see range cattle in this area.
07.3 .. Stay left at a fork before a clearcut.
07.35 Turn left onto a gravel road.
07.6 .. Turn left. Stay straight (left) where two roads come in on the right. There are several other side roads along the next 2.5 miles, but the main route is obvious.
10.2 .. At a fork stay left and head downhill.
10.3 .. Come to the south end of the dam, turn left and cross it.
10.4 .. Turn right onto a somewhat obscure dirt road and after several yards veer left. Come to an old clearcut, turn right and follow the good road through it.
11.0 .. Turn right onto paved Road 42.
12.7 .. Turn right onto Road 240, as indicated by the sign pointing to Clear Lake Butte. Most of the climb is at a moderately steep to steep grade. The pavement ends after 0.7 mile, but the surface continues to be very good.
14.4 .. Stay straight (left) where Road 246 heads to the right.
15.0 .. Come to the summit where you can see, among other landmarks, Mounts Hood and Jefferson, Frog Lake Buttes (No. 11) and Clear and Timothy Lakes.
17.2 .. Descend back to Road 42, turn left and stay on Road 42 all the way to U.S. 26.
19.3 .. Turn left onto U.S. 26. The section of highway between here and Frog Lake is being widened and work is schedule to be completed in 1991, although it may take longer. Before then, schedule the ride for a weekend or, if on a weekday, time it so you come out later in the afternoon when work has stopped.
24.1 .. Turn right into the Frog Lake parking area and come to the end of the ride.

Fire lookout at Clear Lake Butte

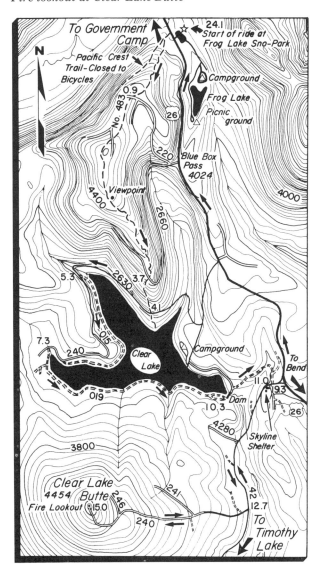

11 FROG LAKE BUTTES LOOP

Difficulty: Moderately hard, primarily because of length
Surface: 0.6 mile on paved roads; 13.4 miles on good, unpaved roads except for one 0.5 mile rough stretch and 2.0 miles on trails (with 1.6 miles of them optional)
Distance: 16 miles round trip (includes trail ride to Catalpa Lake)
Elevation gain: 1,850 feet round trip
High point: 5,294 feet
Usually open July through October

After following a road to the summit of the most southerly of the Frog Lake Buttes south of Mt. Hood this circuit utilizes a short snowmobile trail that connects two roads to complete the loop. An easily optional 1.6 mile (total) side trip along a good cycling trail goes to Catalpa Lake.

From the junction of U.S. 26 and Oregon 35, which is 2.6 miles east of Government Camp, drive south on U.S. 26 for 6.7 miles to signs pointing left to Frog Lake Campground and Sno-Park. Turn into the immense parking area and leave your car here. Outhouses are located at the northeast side.

00.0 .. Begin cycling on paved Road 2610 to Frog Lake that begins from the south side of the parking area.

00.2 .. Turn left onto an unpaved road at the edge of a clearcut and begin climbing at a moderately steep, but comfortable, angle. You'll be returning on the paved road. Soon have the first of many far-ranging views. Just before the 1.0 mile point you can identify lookout-topped Clear Lake Butte (No. 10) to the southwest. From here to the summit the road is bordered by exceptionally fruitful huckleberry bushes.

02.4 .. Stay left at a fork. After you visit the summit, to continue the loop you'll be taking Road 221 to the right. Immediately

begin climbing more steeply along a considerably rougher surface.

03.0 .. Come to the wide summit with its panoramic view. Not surprisingly, a fire lookout tower once stood here.

03.5 .. Return to the junction of Road 221 and follow it east.

04.2 .. Come to the end of the road. The large bodies of water to the southwest are Clear and Timothy Lakes. Walk across the clearcut in the same direction you were heading without losing any elevation for about 150 yards and then follow a wide snowmobile course, which is tagged with orange markers, down through the woods.

04.6 .. Come to the end of Road 250 at another clearcut and turn left onto it. Bonney Butte (No. 15) is the high point on the big ridge to the northeast. Most of the next 5.5 miles is downhill.

05.4 .. Stay straight (left) at the junction of Road 025.

05.7 .. Stay straight (left) at the junction of Road 024.

06.5 .. To make the recommended trail ride to Catalpa Lake turn sharply left onto the road that parallels below the main road. (If you do not intend to make this side trip, pick up the ride at the 8.3 mile point.)

06.6 .. Stay left on the old road bed—do not head down along the signed Barlow Creek Trail No. 471. After 0.1 mile you are automatically funneled onto Trail No. 535 that in a short distance crosses little Green Lake Creek.

07.4 .. Come to the lake tucked at the bottom of a rocky cirque.

08.3 .. Retrace your route to the main road, No. 250, and continue south along it.

09.5 .. Stay straight at an open area where Road 252 heads right.

09.9 .. Turn right onto Road 2610 and climb steeply for only a short distance. This junction is marked by a yield sign. After a 0.5 mile climb from the junction you'll have two more uphill stretches of about 0.7 mile each between the 11.0 and 12.9 mile points, but they are moderately easy grades. Stay on the main road where several spurs head off to the right and left.

15.6 .. Come to the beginning of the pavement and several yards farther stay straight (right) at the signed spur down to Frog Lake Campground.

15.8 .. Stay straight (left) at the junction of the road you took up to Frog Lake Buttes.

16.0 .. Come to the end of the ride.

Mt. Hood from summit of Frog Lake Buttes

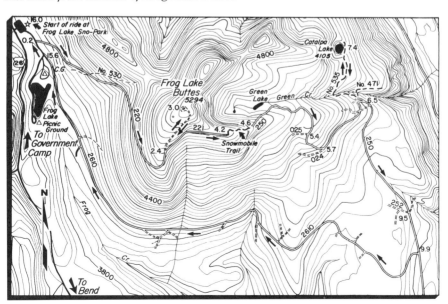

12 BARLOW BUTTE LOOP

Difficulty: Hard because of one stretch down a clearcut and a few overgrown sections of trail.
Surface: 0 mile on paved roads; 10 miles on unpaved roads that range from smooth to rough (but always rideable); 1.5 miles on a sometimes overgrown trail; 0.3 mile of cross-country
Distance: 11.8 miles round trip
Elevation gain: 1,940 feet round trip
High point: 4,700 feet
Usually open July through October

What mountain bikers won't do to make a loop: In this case it's wrestling their bikes down a very steep slope along the edge of a clearcut to an old trail that connects with the roads that complete the circuit. The less energetic can have a fine ride with many viewpoints by just riding to the top of the clearcut at 4.3 miles or by following the Barlow Road and a spur that make up the last 6.3 miles of the loop.

Drive on Oregon 35 for 2.6 miles east of its junction with U.S. 26 or 38 miles south and west of the White Salmon-Government Camp Exit 64 off I-84 just east of Hood River to Barlow Pass Summit at the 60 mile post and turn south, following signs to Pacific Crest Trail and Sno-Park. Take the paved road 0.2 mile to a large parking area.

00.0 ..Cycle south down the rough, unpaved Barlow Road No. 3530, which you passed just before you entered the parking area and is identified by a large, artful wooden sign.
00.1 ..Turn left onto the signed Barlow Butte Trail and Mineral Jane Ski Trail and continue down a narrower road bed.
00.4 ..Turn left at a clearing, continuing on the signed Mineral Jane Ski Trail.
00.45 Stay straight after less than 0.1 mile, following the signed Barlow Butte Trail. Continue climbing for 0.2 mile and

then level off.
00.6 ..Stay straight (left) on the Mineral Jane Ski Trail at the junction of the Barlow Butte Trail, which is too steep for enjoyable cycling.
00.7 ..Stay straight (right) at a minor spur trail to the left.
00.75 Come to unpaved Road 230 and turn left onto it.
01.1 ..Turn right at a T-junction onto Road 3560. The road to the left meets Oregon 35 after 0.2 mile 0.6 mile east of the road to the parking area. Begin 1.6 miles of persistent uphill. At 2.5 miles have a view to Mt. Hood and Mt. Hood Meadows Ski Area (No. 13) and east to Gunsight Ridge (No. 14).
02.7 ..Turn left just beyond where you level off and begin descending on Road 240. The road you were on ends in about 1.7 miles. Stay straight on the main road at several spurs.
04.3 ..Come to the top of the clearcut. You can head down either side. The north (left) route is steeper, but the south (right) side is bushier. At the bottom of the clearcut continue down in the same direction for several yards until you intersect faint Trail No. 538.
04.5 ..Turn right onto the trail and head south.
04.6 ..Continue in the same direction where a path angles back to the left. The tread improves after 0.5 mile, although there is an occasional tree across the route. A couple of hundred feet before you come to the end of the woods at 5.5 miles angle slightly to the right, cross a little bridge with a railing and then bear left 50 feet to a road.
05.5 ..Head south on the road at a mostly gentle downhill grade. Bonney Butte (No. 15) is the high point on the ridge to the left.
06.9 ..Turn right at a 4-way junction onto the Old Barlow Road (No. 3530). Except for a couple of short downhills, mostly climb at a gentle grade, staying straight at all side roads. Cross Barlow Creek at 10.2 miles and recross it 0.3 mile farther at the south end of Devils Half Acre, a meadow considerably larger than its name would suggest.
10.7 ..Stay straight (left) at the junction of Road 220, after 0.1 mile come to the north end of the clearing and begin climbing more noticeably along a rough road.
11.8 ..End of ride at parking area.

Sign at Barlow Pass

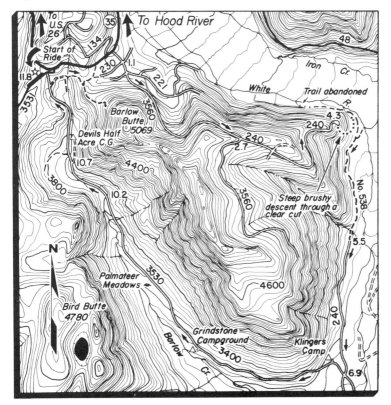

13 MT.HOOD MEADOWS SKI AREA

Difficulty: Hard, because of frequent steep grades
Surface: 0 mile on paved roads; 4.3 miles on unpaved roads, ranging from reasonably smooth to extremely rough; 0 mile on trails
Distance: 2.1 miles one way for the North Route (also described is an optional 2.0 mile round trip side trip); 2.2 miles one way for the South Route
Elevation gain: 1,300 feet for the North Route (an additional 300 feet of uphill for the optional side trip); 1,400 feet for the South Route
High point: 6,700 feet
Usually open August through mid October

Although all but the strongest cyclists will have to walk some portions of the service roads in the Mt. Hood Meadows Ski Area, the routes are entirely rideable on the way down. Two separate trips, which share starting points, are described and they easily can be combined for a one day outing. Arguably the best time to visit is the second to third week in August when the vast expanses of grassy meadows are at their most lush and the wild-flowers are at their peak.

Drive on Oregon 35 for 6.9 miles east of its junction with U.S. 26 or 33.7 miles south and west from the White Salmon-Government Camp Exit 64 off I-84 just east of Hood River to the signed, paved road to Mt. Hood Meadows Ski Area. Turn north and follow the spur 1.9 miles to its end. Park along the shoulders—do not block the gate.

The NORTH ROUTE climbs to the top of the Shooting Star Lift at the edge of immense Clark Creek Canyon.

From the gate ride northeast across the parking area to an unpaved road at about the mid-point along its east side.

00.0 .. Turn onto the dirt road, soon pass tanks and a large, one story storage building and climb through woods.

00.4 .. Stay straight (right), after 0.2 mile come to a crest, curve left on the obvious main road and 0.1 mile farther switch back to the right. You'll have the first of many views south to Mt. Jefferson and North Sister.

01.0 .. Turn left and climb very steeply. The road to the right at this junction is the route of the recommended side trip.

01.5 .. Turn right. The South Route (described below) takes you to the top of the lift to the left.

01.6 .. Turn left at a fork. At 1.9 miles come to signs discussing Heather Canyon. Go to the edge of Clark Creek Canyon for an impressive view.

02.1 .. Come to the top of the Shooting Star Lift.

The recommended 2.0 mile (total) side trip from the junction at 1.0 mile climbs steeply for 0.1 mile and then is more moderate. From the top of the Yellow Lift you can head south to a viewpoint. The main road passes the top of the Hood River Meadows Lift 0.4 mile from the start of the side trip and then descends at a moderate grade along a very good surface for 0.6 mile to the bottom of the Shooting Star Lift.

The SOUTH ROUTE traverses lush meadows that look like a photo of a scene in the Swiss Alps and climbs almost to timberline past the base of the Texas Chair to the top of the Blue Chair at 6,700 feet.

Cycle to the west side of the large parking area and locate the unpaved road that starts from the south side of a one story building. Although the road may be obscured by vehicles and other equipment, once you're on it you'll have no more route-finding problems.

00.0 .. Pass near the lower end of the Butter-cup Lift and climb. Have one short steep pitch, go under the Red Lift at 0.5 mile and 0.6 mile farther ride by the top of it. The road becomes narrower, rougher and steeper be- yond here.

01.3 .. Stay right (downhill) and go under the Daisy Lift. Begin climbing very steeply to the base of the Texas Chair at 2.0 miles. The stream here is a nice spot for a snack stop. Unless you haven't had enough of pushing your bike, leave it here and walk the final 0.2 mile to the aerie-like top of the Blue Lift where you can see to the wheat fields of north-central Oregon. The road below you is one you follow on the North Route ride.

Mt. Hood from Shooting Star Lift

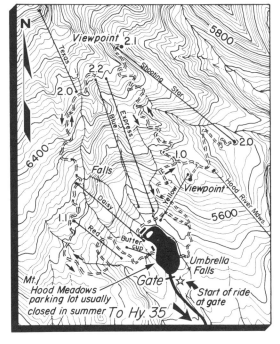

14 GUNSIGHT TRAIL LOOP

Difficulty: Moderately hard
Surface: 0 mile on paved roads; 14.4 miles on unpaved and occasionally rough (but always rideable) roads; 5.3 miles on moderately demanding trails
Distance: 19.7 miles round trip
Elevation gain: 2,900 feet
High point: 6,000 feet
Usually open July through mid October

Cyclists who aren't inclined to do the trail along Gunsight Ridge, located between Bennett Pass and Bonney Butte, can have a thoroughly enjoyable and scenic ride by just following the road portions of this loop. They'll miss the many vistas to the north and northeast along the trail, but still will enjoy the sightings of Badger Lake, Jean Lake and far-ranging scenes to the southeast.

Drive on Oregon 35 for 6.6 miles east of its junction with U.S. 26 or 34 miles south and west from the White Salmon-Government Camp Exit 64 off I-84 just east of Hood River to the large parking area off the southeast side of the highway at Bennett Pass.

00.0 .. Head southeast on the signed Bennett Pass Road, which begins from the northeast end of the parking area.

00.2 .. Stay straight (left) on the main route.

01.1 .. Stay straight (left) and begin a gradual descent.

01.9 .. Stay straight (left). The spur to the right ends in 0.2 mile. Immediately beyond the junction the road becomes narrower and rougher and begins climbing. Cross an open slope on the west side of the ridge where you'll have the first of many good views to the south and then cross to the east side and travel above Pocket Creek

basin (No. 18). After a short downhill section have 1.6 miles of moderate, but persistent, uphill.

04.4 .. Turn left onto the signed west end of the Gunsight Trail No. 685 just a few yards before a T-junction. You'll be returning along the road to the left. The road to the right goes to Bonney Butte and Meadows (No's. 15 and 16). The trail grade moderates after 0.1 mile.

05.0 .. Stay right on the main trail where a path heads down slope. In a short distance switch back and come to the crest. Continue mostly uphill and just before you traverse around the right (east) side of a hump at 6.7 miles you can walk up to the crest for an interesting view of Mt. Hood.

Traverse, descend for a bit and at the end of a short uphill at 7.1 miles look left for a cluster of rocks and walk to its top for a view of Mounts Hood, Adams and Rainier, plus Mt. Hood Meadows Ski Area (No. 13) and Bald Butte (No. 25) above the Upper Hood River Valley. After two short switchbacks have an easy stretch to a talus slope at 7.3 miles and several yards beyond its far end come near the road.

07.4 .. Stay left on the trail. Mostly climb to an open little crest at 7.7 miles that affords views south to Mt. Jefferson, the Three Sisters and the agricultural fields of central Oregon.

07.9 .. Turn left onto the road.

08.1 .. Veer left off the road at the signed resumption of the Gunsight Trail. Traverse an open slope at 9.0 miles and descend in two sets of switchbacks. Continue down along an easy stretch through deep woods.

09.9 .. Come to the road at Gumjuwac Saddle and turn right to continue the loop. The section to the left reaches High Prairie in about 1.9 miles. A recommended lunch stop is to follow Trail No. 480 that heads northeast from where you met the road for just over 0.1 mile to Jack Spring.

After 0.3 mile of steep uphill along the return portion of the ride the road's grade moderates. At 11.5 miles have a steep climb of almost 0.2 mile to the crest and a view down onto Badger Lake. At about 12.3 miles have a view down onto little Jean Lake, which is closed to bicycles.

14.2 .. Stay right at the junction of the road to Badger Lake at Camp Windy.

15.3 .. Turn right onto Road 3550 and retrace your route back.

19.7 .. End of the ride.

36

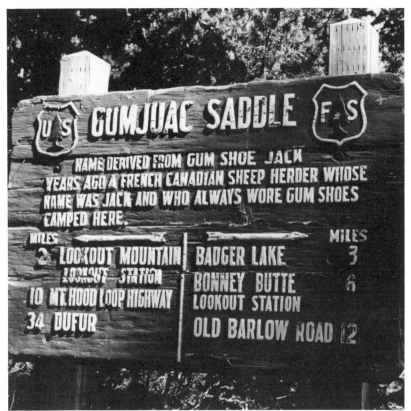

GUMJUAC SADDLE

NAME DERIVED FROM GUM SHOE JACK
YEARS AGO A FRENCH CANADIAN SHEEP HERDER WHOSE
NAME WAS JACK AND WHO ALWAYS WORE GUM SHOES
CAMPED HERE.

MILES ←		→ MILES
2 LOOKOUT MOUNTAIN	BADGER LAKE	3
LOOKOUT STATION		
10 MT. HOOD LOOP HIGHWAY	BONNEY BUTTE	6
	LOOKOUT STATION	
34 DUFUR	OLD BARLOW ROAD	12

Sign at Gumjuwac Saddle

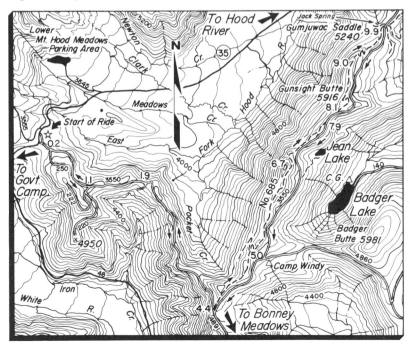

15 BONNEY BUTTE

Difficulty: Moderate
Surface: 0 mile on paved roads; 6.0 miles on unpaved roads with reasonably good surfaces and easy to moderately steep grades, except for 0.2 mile that is very rocky and 0.2 mile that is both very rocky and steep; 0 mile on trails
Distance: 6.0 miles one way
Elevation gain: 1,325 feet; loss 450 feet
High point: 5,550 feet
Usually open July through mid October

Although following roads (the kind you'd rather take your bike on than your car) to Bonney Butte with its panoramic view is an entirely satisfying trip, riders who want a harder outing have several options: The shortest is a 0.5 mile road ride to vast, scenic and lush Bonney Meadows. From there cyclists can make a 7.1 mile loop of moderately easy trail riding (refer to No. 16). You could also combine the ride to Bonney Butte with the one along Gunsight Ridge (No. 14).

Drive on Oregon 35 for 6.6 miles east of its junction with U.S. 26 or 34 miles south and west from the White Salmon-Government Camp Exit 64 off I-84 just east of Hood River to the large parking area off the southeast side of the highway. This point is 0.2 mile south of the spur to Mt. Hood Meadows Ski Area (No. 13).

00.0 ..Head southeast on the signed Bennett Pass Road, which begins from the northeast end of the parking area.

00.2 ..Stay straight (left) on the main road where a narrower route heads right.

01.1 ..Stay straight (left) and descend gradually.

01.9 ..Stay straight (left). The spur to the right ends in 0.2 mile. Immediately beyond the junction the road becomes narrower and rougher and begins climbing. Bikers will have no problems with any of that but they probably will encounter at least one motorist so appalled by the road he'll ask if it really is the way to Badger Lake (it is). Come to an open slope on the west side of the ridge where you'll have good views to the south and then go to the east side and cross a cliff face that ski tourers call the Terrible Traverse. From here you can see ahead to the ridge ride No. 14 follows. The basin of Pocket Creek's drainage directly below is covered on ride No. 18. After a short downhill section have 1.6 miles of moderate, but persistent, uphill.

04.4 ..Turn right onto Road 4891. The trail to the left just before this T-junction and the road to the left are part of ride No. 14. Have an easy traverse for 0.2 mile and then begin climbing along a very rocky road. In 0.2 mile the grade changes to gently downhill, but the surface is even worse.

05.5 ..Turn right onto Road 130. After 0.2 mile of very rough, but levelish road begin 0.3 mile of very steep uphill. Most people will have to walk much of this final stretch.

06.0 ..Come to the summit, the site of a former fire lookout. The view extends from Mounts Adams and Hood south along the crest of the Cascades to Mt. Jefferson and southeast over the Tygh Valley to Juniper Butte (the Smith Rocks area) in central Oregon. Bonney Meadows is directly below and to the west are Barlow (No. 12) and Frog Lake (No. 11) Buttes and beyond them the Multorpor—Ski Bowl ski areas (No. 6).

If you want to visit Bonney Meadows retrace your route the 0.5 mile to Road 4891 and turn right. Follow the road 0.3 mile to the signed spur that heads left to Bonney Meadows Campground. Note there is a cattle guard in several hundred feet. After 0.2 mile along the spur stay left where the road forks (since this is part of the little loop through the campground, you could also turn right here) and follow it past the start of the Boulder Lake Trail to the start of the signed Forest Creek Trail. If you're planning to make the fun trail loop, angle directly across Bonney Meadows to the edge of the trees (this is at the 3.2 mile point in the log for No. 16).

Mt. Hood from Bonney Butte

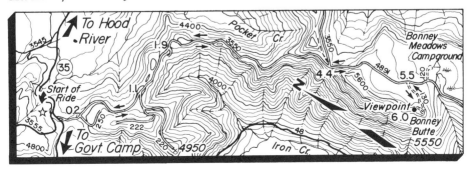

16 BONNEY MEADOWS LOOP

Difficulty: Moderate
Surface: 0 mile on paved roads; 1.1 miles on good unpaved roads; 6.0 miles on gently to moderately graded, good trails (except for 0.3 mile of steep uphill)
Distance: 7.1 miles round trip
Elevation gain: 1,550 feet round trip
High point: 5,450 feet
Usually open July through October

The turnaround point of this moderately easy trail ride is vast Bonney Meadows, with its lush expanse and picture perfect view of Mt. Hood making it arguably the best looking clearing in the area. During 1989, the original southernmost end of this loop was obliterated by a logging operation. However, if this trail has been rebuilt you could take it from the 6.0 mile point back to the start, instead of following roads. Other options include a 2.2 mile (round trip) side excursion to Bonney Butte (No. 15), a 1.8 mile (round trip) visit to Little Boulder Lake or combining the Bonney Butte and Bonney Meadows routes.

Drive on Oregon 35 for 4.9 miles east of its junction with U.S. 26 or 35.7 miles south from the White Salmon-Government Camp Exit 64 off I-84 just east of Hood River to the east side of the White River Sno-Park and turn south on paved Road 48. After 11.4 miles turn left onto paved Road 4890 and 1.9 miles farther turn right onto Road 4881. After 0.6 mile turn left onto unpaved Road 120, in 1.4 miles turn right onto Road 121, 0.5 mile farther, at the junction of Road 122, stay right, continuing on Road 121, and in 0.2 mile come to the start of the ride. A clearcut is on the right and the road is in the middle of a curve to the left. Look for a sign (perhaps still one of those temporary yellow kind) identifying the Hidden Meadows Trail No.

472 to the left (north). If you're interested in taking the trail all the way back, check south across the road to see if the tread has been rebuilt.

00.0 .. Head north through woods at a level to gentle uphill grade.

00.3 .. Turn right where you come to Road 122 and after .04 mile look for a yellow sign on the left and ride through the clearcut.

00.9 .. Come to Road 122 again, cross it and continue in the same direction across a logged area, looking ahead 200 feet for a trail sign. Begin climbing more noticeably at 1.8 miles. From 2.1 to 2.2 miles have a very steep stretch past dense huckleberry bushes and then resume the moderate uphill. At 2.5 miles begin 0.3 mile of level and at 2.6 miles pass the upper end of Road 122 several yards off to the left. (On the drive in you passed the south end of this 2.5 mile spur 0.2 mile before the trailhead.) Continue on the level trail for another 0.2 mile and then descend for 0.1 mile to near Bonney Meadows.

02.9 .. Stay right where the trail forks and follow along the eastern edge of the meadow.

03.2 .. Turn right onto the Forest Creek Trail No. 473. (To visit Bonney Butte, turn left and head directly across the clearing.) Climb steeply for 0.2 mile to the crest of Echo Point where you'll have views into central Oregon and northeast to Gunsight Ridge (No. 14). Head south at a levelish to gentle downhill grade, initially past more dense huckleberry bushes. (You have the option of leaving the trail at the 4.2 mile point, just before the lower end of a clearcut on your right. Head directly west across the logged area for several hundred yards to Road 121, turn left and follow it down for 1.6 miles to the 6.2 mile point of the log.)

Continue along the trail, generally near the edge of the breaks except for one stretch through a clearcut. At 5.0 miles pass an imposing, rocky overlook above Little Boulder Lake. At 5.8 miles pass another clearcut.

06.0 .. Come to Road 123 and turn right. (If you're taking the trail all the way back, look for the resumption of the tread across the road. To visit Little Boulder Lake, turn left, immediately turn left again and descend along Road 123 for 0.9 mile.)

06.2 .. Turn left at the junction of Road 121.

07.1 .. End of the ride.

Bonney Meadows

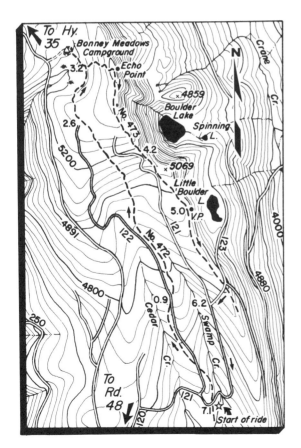

To Hy. 35
Bonney Meadows Campground
3.2
Echo Point
x 4859
Boulder Lake
Spinning L.
2.6
No. 473
5200
4.2
x 5069
Little Boulder L.
5.0
V.P.
4891
122
No. 472
121
123
4000
4880
4800
0.9
6.2
Cedar Cr.
Swamp Cr.
250
To Rd. 48
121
7.1
Start of ride
1201
N
Crane Cr.

41

17 GRASSHOPPER POINT— ROCKY BUTTE LOOP

Difficulty: Moderately hard, because of 0.2 mile of steep, rough road and 0.3 mile of steep trail
Surface: 0.5 mile on paved roads; 6.5 miles on mostly good unpaved roads; 2.4 miles on mostly good trails
Distance: 9.4 miles round trip
Elevation gain: 1,545 feet round trip
High point: 5,385 feet
Usually open July through October

Not only are both Grasshopper Point and Rocky Butte superb viewpoints, they also face opposite directions—the first west with sightings along the Cascades from Mt. Hood through Mt. Jefferson and the second east down onto the Tygh Valley and beyond. Assuming there is no blowdown, the only sections of trail that are not easy going are the several hundred yards of steep grades on either side of Rocky Butte. And the one rough section of road is rideable for most of its distance.

Drive on Oregon 35 for 4.9 miles east of its junction with U.S. 26 or 35.7 miles south and west of the White Salmon-Government Camp Exit 64 off I-84 just east of Hood River to the east side of the White River Sno-Park and turn south onto paved Road 48. After 11.4 miles stay straight at a 4-way junction, continue on Road 48 for another 4.1 miles and turn left onto Road 4860. Its surface is graveled for only a short distance. After 3.5 miles come to the end of the pavement at the junction of Road 130 and park here.

00.0 .. Continue north along Road 4860 at a mostly uphill grade.
00.3 .. Stay straight where Road 180 heads off to the left. (At about 1.0 mile an abandoned road—not taken by the authors—heads left at an obscure junction, offering an alternative route to Grasshopper Point.)
02.0 .. Turn left onto the Rocky Butte Trail No. 475 that follows along the south side of a new clearcut.
02.2 .. Turn left onto a road.

02.25 Turn right at a fork. The road becomes increasingly faint, but it's no problem to follow out to Grasshopper Point at 2.4 miles. Clear Lake Butte (No. 10) and the ridge the ride to Squaw Mountain (No. 32) follows are to the southwest and nearby to the west are Gunsight Ridge (No. 14) and Bonney Butte (No. 15). Retrace your route to the Road 4860.
02.8 .. Head downhill (east) from the 2.0 mile point along the trail that continues along the south side of a clearcut.
03.4 .. Turn left onto a road at a clearcut.
03.5 .. Turn right at a T-junction.
03.6 .. Turn left onto the resumption of the trail. (Note that the trail through the clearcut you meet at 3.4 miles may be rebuilt. However, also note that the trail that continues directly across the road at 3.4 miles in the same direction you were heading and then doubles back to the right after 0.2 mile is not the route you want.) Pass a little meadow at 3.7 miles and then come to a clearcut. You may have to walk for .05 mile.
03.9 .. Cross a road to the resumption of the trail. If the blowdown on the route has not been cleared, go around the debris on the right. Begin 0.2 mile of very steep uphill at 4.4 miles.
04.6 .. Come to the top of Rocky Butte. Walk to the rocks on the east side for the best view, including a view beyond the canyon of the Deschutes River to eastern Oregon.

Follow the trail that continues down the west and south sides of Rocky Butte. The grade is steep at first but becomes less so the farther you descend.
05.0 .. Turn left onto Road 4812.
05.9 .. Turn right at the T-junction with Road 4811.
06.1 .. Turn right onto paved Road 4813 at a 4-way junction and begin a moderate climb, except for one short downhill. At 6.6 miles the pavement and the uphill both end. At 6.9 miles pass Bell Spring and at 7.4 miles cross Gate Creek where there is a small picnic spot.
07.6 .. Turn right onto Road 130. After 0.8 mile, just beyond where the surface becomes rougher, curve gently left where a faint bed (No. 017) comes in on the right. By 8.6 miles the grade lessens and in another 0.1 mile the surface improves considerably. At 9.3 miles curve right.
09.4 .. Come to your starting point.

Rocky Butte Viewpoint

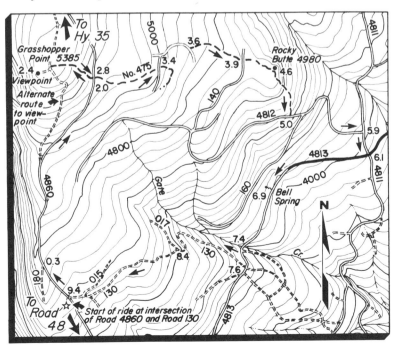

18 POCKET CREEK LOOP

Difficulty: Moderate
Surface: 3.3 miles on paved roads; 10.1 miles on good, unpaved roads; 0.1 mile on trails; 0.7 mile of alternating walking and cycling
Distance: 14.2 miles round trip
Elevation gain: 1,400 feet round trip
High point: 4,800 feet
Usually open late June through October

From Oregon 35 the Pocket Creek area doesn't seem all that enticing but, in fact, it's a maze of roads that wend through unexpectedly varied terrain. In order to explore this basin as a loop trip, you'll have to alternate between walking and cycling for a level 0.7 mile. However, almost all of this stroll is past very dense huckleberry bushes, whose abundant fruit ripens the second half of August.

Drive on Oregon 35 for 10.1 miles east of its junction with U.S. 26 or 30.5 miles south and west from the White Salmon-Government Camp Exit 64 off I-84 just east of Hood River to the Pocket Creek Sno-Park off the south side of the highway at the 67 mile post and park here.

00.0 ..Head southeast from the east end of the parking area on paved 3540.
00.4 ..Stay straight (left) at the junction of unpaved Road 620, which you will be returning on if you make the suggested loop. In 0.2 mile cross the East Fork of the Hood River and begin climbing. Beginning at about 1.3 miles you'll be able to see ahead to the "Terrible Traverse" section of rides No's. 14 and 15. A bit farther you'll have your first views of nearby Mt. Hood, photogenically framed by larch trees and at 2.5 miles come to a crest.
02.9 ..Turn left onto Road 640, which traverses high on the south and east walls of Pocket Creek basin, and concurrently come to the end of the pavement. This recommended side trip provides a fun coast back, plus there are sightings of Mt. Adams. At 3.7 miles pass a waterfall and an exquisite mossy rock wall.
05.0 ..Reach the end of the road and retrace your route to the 2.9 mile point.
07.2 ..Turn left onto Road 3540 and resume the easy uphill for 1.0 mile, have 0.5 mile of downhill and then climb for a final 0.1 mile to just yards before the road abruptly becomes steeper and very rough.
08.9 Look for a "More Difficult" cross-country ski marker on your right. Turn right, veer left and follow the trail that parallels below the road. In a couple of hundred feet pass a sign identifying the Teacup Lake Trail. The route is reasonably obvious, but if you have doubts just follow the diamond-shaped blue ski markers. After a long 0.6 mile cross a pole bridge. Continue in the same direction you were heading for 100 feet or so, cross a cat road and immediately come to Road 680.
09.6 ..Turn right and travel on the level or gently downhill for 1.2 miles and then have 0.1 mile of uphill.
10.9 ..Turn right (downhill). (If you want to skip this next section, you can stay left and in just over 0.1 mile come to where the route described below rejoins the road at 11.7 miles in the log.)
11.3 ..Turn left where a sign points to Raven's Run Lodge and then after a few yards turn left again onto a bumpy road, following the black and white ski markers.
11.7 ..Turn right onto Road 680 you turned off of at 10.9 miles.
11.8 ..Turn right onto Road 681 and travel on the level, staying straight (right) where two roads head off to the left.
12.0 ..Turn right at a T-junction, continuing on duffy Road 681.
12.5 ..Turn left at the sign identifying the Meadows Creek Trail, after 0.1 mile cross Clark Creek on a wide pole bridge and continue in the same direction for a couple of hundred feet to Road 620.
12.7 ..Turn left.
12.75 Turn right at a T-junction, staying on Road 620.
13.0 ..Stay straight (right) where a sandy road goes left and continue the easy downhill.
13.8 ..Turn left onto paved Road 3540 you took in.
14.2 ..Come to the end of the ride at Oregon 35.

Waterfall along road

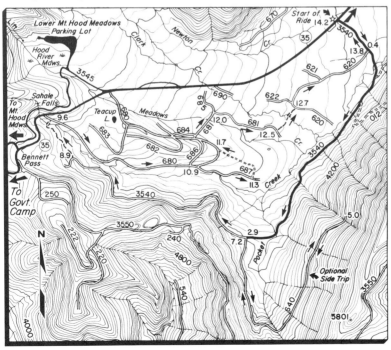

45

19 KNEBAL SPRINGS— PERRY POINT LOOP

Difficulty: Moderate
Surface: 2.2 miles on paved roads; 0.5 mile on unpaved roads; 7.4 miles on mostly good trails
Distance: 10.1 miles round trip
Elevation gain: 2,400 feet round trip
High point: 5,020 feet
Usually open mid June through October

All levels of cyclists will enjoy this loop east of Mt. Hood that mostly follows trails through a variety of coniferous woods and past clearcuts to a rocky high point: The experienced can zoom along and those relatively new to trail riding will have few problems because the tread is mostly smooth, gently graded and reasonably wide. As with ride No. 20, which shares the same starting point, this trip is even better done after a day or two of rain because of the occasional sections of very duffy soil.

Drive on Oregon 35 for 14.1 miles east of its junction with U.S. 26 or 26.5 miles south from the White Salmon-Government Camp Exit 64 off I-84 just east of Hood River to Road 44. Turn northeast and stay on paved Road 44 for 7.3 miles to the sign on the north (left) identifying the start of the Knebal Springs Trail. Park in the flat area off the south side of the road.

00.0 ..Head north from the trail sign.
00.1 ..Cross a road and have a couple of short steep uphill stretches.
01.0 ..Cross a road.
01.3 ..Turn right onto a road and follow it for .01 mile, enjoying views of Mounts Hood and Adams, to the resumption of the trail. Except for one short steep descent, the grade is gradually downhill until the low point at Knebal Springs Campground at 4.3 miles.

01.8 ..Come to a road, turn left and take it 75 feet.
01.85 Turn right onto the resumption of the trail.
02.2 ..Come to a road, veer only a few yards to the right and pick up the trail across the bed.
02.3 ..Turn right onto paved Road 1720.
04.1 ..Turn right onto unpaved Road 150.
04.3 ..Follow the road as it curves left after entering the camp area at Knebel Springs. Note the trough and flowing, fresh water on your left as you make that turn.
04.4 ..Turn right onto the obvious trail, which is marked by a sign identifying it as the Knebel Springs Trail No. 474. Have an easy climb to a crest at 4.6 miles, descend for 0.3 mile to a stream crossing and then traverse uphill for 0.5 mile, the only side-hilling along the loop.
05.6 ..Turn left onto a spur road and follow it for .07 mile.
05.65 Turn right onto the obvious, but possibly unsigned, continuation of Trail 474 that is identified by a big, new blaze on a tree. Cross an old road at 5.9 miles.
06.1 ..Turn right onto the Bottle Prairie Trail No. 455 at a T-junction. Initially, continue at the easy grade, but farther on begin climbing more noticeably. Around 6.2 miles ride on an old road for a short distance and then resume traveling on a trail. At 6.8 miles look left for a glimpse of the fire lookout on Fivemile Butte.
07.0 ..Cross a dirt road.
07.2 ..Cross another dirt road.
07.8 ..Veer right onto an old logging road at a clearcut and then stay straight along the edge of the clearcut where the road curves right—all this is obvious in the field.
08.8 ..About 0.1 mile after you've curved left (south) onto a crest look for a path on your left and a sign facing the other way identifying this as the spur to Perry Point. It heads on the level for 0.1 mile to another view of Fivemile Butte and down onto the Dufur Valley. The main route descends to a meadow where the trail widens to an old dirt road.
09.5 ..Come to a T-junction and turn left.
09.6 ..Turn right and then left and head the couple of hundred feet to the paved road.
09.7 ..Turn right onto Road 44. The dirt road across 44 is the route of ride No. 20.
10.1 ..End of the ride.

Fivemile Butte from Perry Point

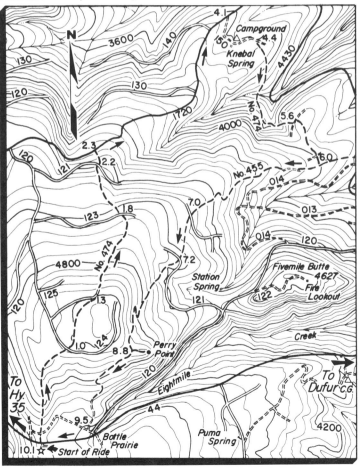

20 FLAG POINT

Difficulty: Moderate
Surface: 2.3 miles on paved roads; 3.8 miles on good unpaved roads; 4.6 miles on excellent trails; option of returning along paved (or some unpaved) roads, which is the same distance as by trail
Distance: 10.7 miles one way
Elevation gain: 1,700 feet; loss 600 feet
High point: 5,640 feet
Usually open late June through October

If you've never done any sustained trail riding or you're introducing someone to it, this route on the east side of the Cascades between Mt. Hood and Tygh Valley is perfect with its smooth, wide, mostly gently graded treads. And as if that weren't enough, the panoramas from the fire lookout (one of the few that is still staffed) and a second viewpoint near the destination are superb. Contrary to most rides, this one is even better after a day or two of rain because of the duffy trails.

Drive on Oregon 35 for 14.1 miles east of its junction with U.S. 26 or 26.5 miles south from the White Salmon-Government Camp Exit 64 off I-84 just east of Hood River to Road 44, the Dufur Mill Road. Turn northeast, following the sign to Camp Baldwin, and stay on paved Road 44 for 7.3 miles to the sign on the north (left) identifying the start of the Knebal Springs Trail (No. 19). Park in the flat area off the south side of the road.

00.0 ..Continue east along Road 44.

00.4 ..Turn right onto a dirt road at the sign pointing to Lookout Mountain Trail. Have only a short uphill stretch and then travel on the level. After 0.4 mile the road narrows into a trail.

02.4 ..Stay straight (right) where the signed Wampus Springs Trail heads left.

03.1 ..Stay straight (left) where the Fifteenmile Trail heads right.

03.15 Turn left on a road and head gently downhill.

03.2 ..Turn left off the road onto a trail (the illegible remains of a sign on the right

identifies the resumption of the route).

03.3 ..Cross a road.

03.4 ..Cross a road, climb past Eightmile Point and at 5.0 miles enter a clearcut.

05.1 ..Turn left onto a dirt road and in .05 mile come to a paved road. The final 100 feet or so in the clearcut are vague so you may meet the paved—actually an oiled—road directly.

05.15 Turn right on the paved road and head downhill. Fifteenmile Forest Camp (which has outhouses) that you pass at 5.6 miles is the start of ride No. 21.

07.0 ..Turn right onto an unpaved road identified by the sign pointing to Flag Point Lookout and climb at a moderate grade, which, uncharacteristically, becomes even more gentle beyond the 9.0 mile point. At 7.9 miles pass Three Bear Spring on your right.

09.9 ..Stay straight (right) at a fork. Note that these roads are in a corridor through a portion of the Badger Creek Wilderness and that the trails to the left and right are closed to bicycles. Go around a gate at 10.4 miles. Just as you curve left to reach the base of the lookout tower look for an unsigned trail on your right. Now, or after visiting the lookout, follow the level path (which is not in the preserve) 0.1 mile to an outstanding viewpoint directly down into the Badger Creek Wilderness and to landmarks to the southwest.

10.7 ..Come to the lookout. If the steps are not gated, climb to the top where you'll enjoy views of Mounts Adams and Jefferson and nearby Mt. Hood, down onto Tygh Valley and, on exceptionally clear days, east to the Blue Mountains. The big body of water to the southeast is Pine Hollow Reservoir.

Retrace your route to the 5.1 mile point (16.3 miles if you're measuring round trip distance) where you first met the paved road.

If you plan to take roads back, continue along No. 2730, enjoying views to the northeast. (As the map shows, you also could take unpaved Road 240, which parallels below Road 2730, for most of the distance back to Road 44. Note that 240 was not ridden by the authors.) At 18.0 miles stay right on paved Road 4420, at 19.3 miles stay left at the junction of Road 4421 and at 20.3 miles come to Road 44. Turn left and ride the final 1.5 miles to your starting point.

The lookout

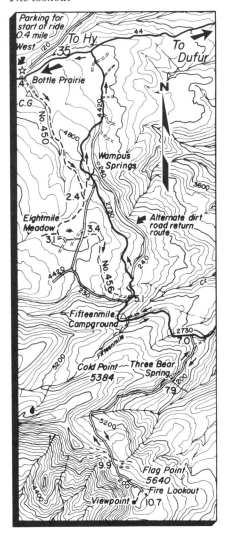

Parking for
start of ride
0.4 mile
West
To Hy.
44
To
Dufur
120
.35
Bottle Prairie
.4
N
C.G.
No. 450
4420
4800
Wampus
Springs
No. 240
2730
3600
2.4
Alternate dirt
road return
route.
Eightmile
Meadow
3.4
3.1
No. 456
240
4420
230
5.1
CF
Fifteenmile
Campground
2730
7.0
Fifteenmile
3200
Cold Point
5384
Three Bear
Spring
1200
7.9
5200
9.9
Flag Point
5640
4400
200
Fire Lookout
Viewpoint
10.7

21 FIFTEENMILE CREEK LOOP

Difficulty: Moderately hard
Surface: 0 mile on paved roads; 0.8 mile on unpaved roads; 10.7 miles on mostly good trails
Distance: 11.5 miles round trip
Elevation gain: 1,950 feet round trip
High point: 5,650 feet
Usually open late June through October

Except for 0.8 mile along an amusingly rough old road, the Fifteenmile Creek Loop is entirely on trails. People new to trail riding who have enjoyed the other two routes in the area (No's. 19 and 20) should be able to manage this one with no problem. The circuit, which is downhill on the way in, travels through a variety of woods and passes several good viewpoints.

Most riders will have to walk up much of a 1.0 mile stretch at the beginning of the return climb. However, the remainder of the ride back is along an excellent cycling trail and making the loop in the clockwise direction described below is recommended. Because of the two fords of Fifteenmile Creek, the ride is best done after late June when the heaviest snow runoff usually is over, although even then you'll still probably get your shoes wet.

Drive on Oregon 35 for 14.1 miles east of its junction with U.S. 26 or 26.5 miles south from the White Salmon-Government Camp Exit 64 off I-84 just east of Hood River to Road 44. Turn northeast and stay on paved Road 44 (passing the start of No's. 19 and 20 after 7.3 miles) for 8.6 miles to paved Road 4420 to Flag Point Lookout. Turn right, after 0.9 miles stay right on 4420 and 1.2 miles farther keep straight (left) on Road 2730. Drive the final 2.0 miles to Fifteenmile Forest Camp and park here. The signed trail, No. 456, begins between the outhouse and Road 2730.

00.0 .. Descend along the trail that narrows after a few hundred yards.

00.5 .. Stay straight (left) on No. 456 at the junction of No. 457, your return route. Continue down at an increasingly moderate grade. Cross a little stream at 1.2 miles and climb for 0.2 mile to a viewpoint. Have a series of ups and downs through more open woods.

01.7 .. Turn left at a trail sign, as indicated by the arrow, and begin traveling on a levelish old road that is rougher than any of the trails. The surface improves after about 0.3 mile.

02.5 .. Turn right onto Trail No. 456 at a small wooden sign low on a tree on your right. Be alert for this somewhat obscure junction.

03.0 .. Stay right at a fork and head downhill. The spur to the left goes to a road. Farther on begin traveling at a very gentle grade and cross another small stream at 4.0 miles. Continue along the easy grade through woods that in October are brightened with turning maple and other deciduous vegetation.

06.0 .. Turn right at a campsite at the junction of the lower end of Cedar Creek Trail No. 457 (the sign for which is facing the other way). This crucial junction is in a little flat, open area right next to Fifteenmile Creek and there are two sets of trail signs, one on the ground and one on a tree.

Ford Fifteenmile Creek and after a brief easy stretch begin that 1.0 mile of steep, rocky uphill. The scenic surroundings and the promise of 4.0 miles of superb trail riding to come are pleasing distractions.

07.6 .. Cross a road. A set of short, but steep, switchbacks at 7.7 miles is the only interruption to the good riding. At 8.1 miles cross over a broad crest where you can see the tip of Mt. Hood and then have 0.3 mile of easy downhill to a view across the canyon holding Fifteenmile Creek to Mt. Adams.

10.5 .. Turn right. (As the sign here indicates, you can also stay straight and meet Road 2730, the one that goes by the Forest Camp where you started.) Descend along a narrower and rougher tread to the ford of Fifteenmile Creek and climb several yards to the trail you took in.

11.0 .. Turn left and retrace your route.

11.5 .. Come to the end of the ride.

Viewpoint at 1.4 miles

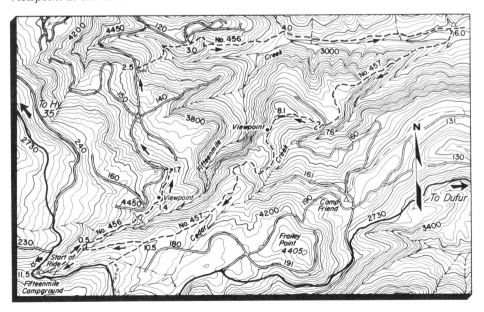

22 CLOUD CAP ROAD— TILLY JANE SKI TRAIL LOOP

Difficulty: Moderate
Surface: 0 mile on paved roads; 9.8
miles on good unpaved roads;
3.5 miles on mostly smooth
trails
Distance: 13.3 miles round trip
Elevation gain: 2,200 feet round trip
High point: 5,900 feet
Usually open July through mid October

After a moderately easy 9.5 mile road climb through a fine alpine landscape to the first structure built on Mt. Hood this loop returns along a more challenging, and considerably shorter, cross-country ski trail. Although a few sections of the descent can be managed (and savored) only by hot doggers, much of it is rideable by all and those portions that need to be walked afford a leisurely opportunity to enjoy the scenery. If you're passing a ranger station that is open on the drive in, pick up a copy of the informative brochure on the Cloud Cap—Tilly Jane Auto Tour.

Drive on Oregon 35 for 16.6 miles east and north of its junction with U.S. 26 or 24 miles south of the White Salmon-Government Camp Exit 64 off I-84 just east of Hood River and turn north onto Cooper Spur Road. After 2.4 miles turn left, following the sign to Cooper Spur Ski Area, 1.4 miles farther stay straight (right) at the one way entrance loop to the ski area and follow unpaved Road 3512 for a few hundred feet to a turnout on your right. You'll be coming out on the signed Tilly Jane Ski Trail across the road.

00.0 .. Cycle along Road 3512. The shortcuts (identified by blue diamond cross-country ski markers) between the first two sets of switchbacks are not much fun to take because of the many downed logs. At 3.4 miles come to the first switchback at

Inspiration Point, which offers an impressive view of Mt. Hood and Wallalute Falls. A 50 yard long trail heads down from the turn to a view with a different perspective.

Wind up in a series of long switchbacks over the next 4.8 miles. Just before the one to the left at 7.6 miles you'll have a bird's-eye view down over the Upper Hood River Valley and a portion of the Lower. Three of the high points on the ridges to the east are destinations of rides in this guide: Surveyors Ridge (No. 24), Bald Butte (No. 25) and Hood River Mountain (No. 29).

08.7 .. Turn right at a T-junction. The road to the left goes to Tilly Jane Campground, which you eventually will be going through, but first you'll want to visit Cloud Cap Inn.

09.4 .. Pass Cloud Cap Saddle Campground on your right where a sign points to Timberline Trail. You'll be turning in here after the visit to Cloud Cap Inn.

09.6 .. End of the road near the former Cloud Cap Inn, which celebrated its 100th birthday in 1989. However, don't get your hopes up for refreshments, because it hasn't been open to the public for 50 years.

09.8 .. Return to the sign pointing to Timberline Trail and head due south through the camp area for a couple of hundred feet to signs. Turn sharply left onto the trail to Tilly Jane (Do Not turn onto the Timberline Trail, which is closed to bicycles) and begin a gentle descent.

10.2 .. Stay left (straight) where a trail heads right.

10.3 .. Turn right at Tilly Jane Campground. Head south, keeping the green building on your right as you pass it, follow a trail in and out of the little canyon holding Tilly Jane Creek and go past an amphitheater.

10.4 .. Stay straight (left) where a trail heads right, pass two buildings on your right and just beyond the second one come to the signed beginning of the Tilly Jane Ski Trail No. 643. As you continue down, the trail tends to become increasingly smoother and less steep.

12.5 .. Turn left just before the crossing of Doe Creek. A sign here points ahead to Cooper Spur Ski Area. Behind you is a sign pointing to Road S12 (the old number) Parking. Head down the little valley and after 0.5 mile pass through a short boggy stretch.

13.3 .. Come to Road 3512 and the end of the ride.

Mt. Hood from Inspiration Point

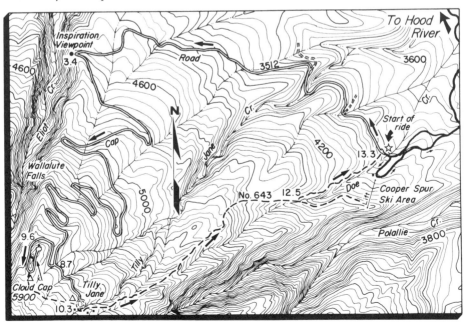

23 RED HILL

Difficulty: Moderate
Surface: 6.8 miles on paved roads; 4.2 miles on unpaved roads; 0 mile on cycling trails; 1.3 miles of hiking
Distance: 11 miles one way of cycling; 1.3 miles one way of hiking
Elevation gain: 2,900 feet of cycling; 550 feet gain and 250 feet loss of hiking
High point: 4,950 feet
Usually open late June through October

From the bucolic setting of the Upper Hood River Valley, this ride climbs along a paved forest road (which affords a superb descent on the return), turns onto a gravel road and then takes one of cobblestone-like rocks that provides the kind of weird fun mountain bikers enjoy to an excellent viewpoint. This is an entirely satisfying turnaround point for people who don't want to hike the additional 1.3 miles to Red Hill.

If you're approaching on I-84, take the White Salmon-Government Camp Exit 64 just east of Hood River, turn right and then immediately right again, following signs to Oregon 35 and Government Camp. Continue on Oregon 35 for 13.5 miles to the community of Mt. Hood and turn right onto the road to Parkdale. After 1.8 miles turn right, in 0.2 mile turn right at the Parkdale Work Center of the Mt. Hood National Forest and park in front of the building. If you're coming from the west on Oregon 35 take it for 23 miles from its junction with U.S. 26 to the road to Parkdale. This junction is just north of the 80 mile post. After 2.3 miles turn left and go the 0.2 mile to the Work Center on your right.

00.0 .. Head west toward the center of Parkdale.
00.4 .. Stay straight (left), following the sign to Baseline Road. Be alert here because you'll be crossing a busy road.

01.1 .. Curve right on Old Parkdale Road.
01.4 .. Turn left onto Red Hill Drive. Around 1.9 miles have the first views of the Parkdale Lava Flow on your left. Near the 2.0 mile point the road narrows, becoming Forest Road 16, and 0.4 mile farther the almost unremitting, but never steep, uphill begins. Continue on paved Road 16 at all side roads. You'll be looking ahead to Mt. Hood along a good portion of the ride and at 5.7 miles you'll have a view down onto the Upper Hood River Valley and across to Surveyors Ridge (No. 24) and Bald Butte (No. 25). Note the 4-way junction at 6.7 miles of Roads 1610 and 1620 because the road you want to turn onto is just beyond it.
06.8 .. Turn left onto unpaved Road 1630.
07.5 .. Stay right on Road 1630. Come to another good viewpoint at 7.9 miles and have a short downhill stretch.
09.1 .. Turn left onto a rough, unnumbered road (No. 660 on the map) that looks like it should end in a short distance. Don't worry about missing this turn because just over 0.1 mile beyond it along the main road is a T-junction with Road 1631. After several yards the side route curves left, then right and levels off before resuming climbing. At 10.7 miles look to your right for the path to wee Perry Lake.
11.0 .. Come to the first foundation of the Tony Creek Guard Station and that promised panorama. You'll now also be able to see Mounts St. Helens and Rainier, Mt. Defiance (No. 28) and other landmarks in the Columbia River Gorge and the terrain of the southern Washington Cascades.

If you intend to hike the initially rocky trail to Red Hill, continue along the road to just beyond a second, larger foundation and stay straight on a trail. Climb to a crest, descend through woods into a meadow and turn right at its center. (The meadow off to your left during the drop is not the one you want.) Follow the swale for about 300 feet to where it curves left. Veer right here and begin climbing. Note landmarks because it's recommended that you follow precisely the same route back. About 200 yards from where you began climbing come to the open area just below the ridge crest, turn left (west) and go the final few hundred yards to the summit, walking along the upper edge of the red pumice so you don't leave footprints that would mar the terrain.

Mt. Hood from Red Hill

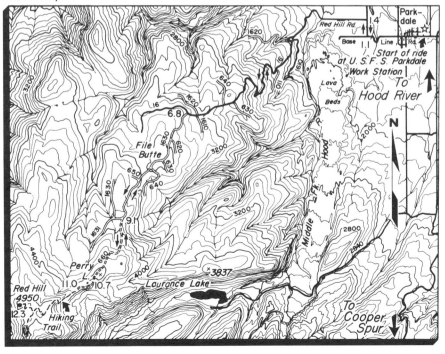

55

24 SURVEYORS RIDGE LOOP

Difficulty: Very hard
Surface: 14.8 miles on paved roads; 1.3 miles on unpaved roads; 20.5 miles on trails or narrow dirt roads (some sections of trails rough or very steep, but overall good grades and surfaces)
Distance: 36.6 miles round trip
Elevation gain: 3,700 feet round trip
High point: 4,280 feet
Usually open late June through October

This loop, the hardest in the guide, combines roads and trails both in and south of the Upper Hood River Valley. By studying the ride map and the recreation map for the Mt. Hood National Forest, you can create shorter and/or easier variations.

Follow Oregon 35 for 14 miles south of Exit 64 off I-84 just east of Hood River or 26.6 miles east and north from U.S. 26 to the Hood River Ranger Station 0.4 mile south of the community of Mt. Hood. Park in the open area south of the building. This is also the start of ride No. 25.

00.0 .. Head south on Oregon 35, which has a good shoulder.

05.1 .. Turn left onto a narrow dirt road at a sign stating Dog River Trail No. 675.

05.2 .. Stay right at a fork and after few hundred feet veer right onto a trail and cross Puppy Creek on a bridge. Have an easy ford of the Dog River at 7.2 miles, at 8.5 miles pass a rocky viewpoint and soon climb very steeply in four "killer" switchbacks.

08.9 .. Stay right at a fork to Road No. 620.

09.4 .. Switch back right and soon descend, passing a spring at 10.4 miles.

11.2 .. Turn left onto Trail No. 678.

12.0 .. Turn left at an old road. You've now gained about 70 per cent of the elevation.

12.2 .. Come to Road 620 and cross it to a level old roadbed. Road 44 is several yards to the right and from here it is 3.7 miles down to its junction with Oregon 35.

13.2 .. Veer left off the road onto a signed trail just before you come to Road 17. Stay left at the junction of the Cooks Meadow

Trail, have an easy ford—the last source of water—and cross a meadow.

14.0 .. Stay left on a sometimes duffy logging road.

16.4 .. Turn left onto the signed Surveyors Ridge Trail. This junction is at the low side of a clearcut and 0.15 mile before the junction with Road 17, which connects with Road 44.

17.3 .. Come to a gravel road and cross it. At 19.6 miles pass a signed path on your left to Shellrock Mountain.

20.2 .. Come to an old road and turn left.

20.25 Veer left onto a trail just before a gravel road. Traverse mostly up along a rough trail and cross over a crest at 20.7 miles.

21.3 .. Come to a gate and beyond it stay left.

21.5 .. Turn left onto a narrow, dirt road and climb steeply for 0.3 mile. At 22.1 miles, walk left to the former site of the Rim Rock Lookout that affords the best of the many excellent panoramas along this ride.

22.4 .. Cross a road.

22.7 .. Come to a road, turn left, and go about 50 feet.

22.75 Turn right onto the resumption of the trail on the other side of an up-turned stump.

23.5 .. Turn right at a T-junction. The spur to the left ends at an excellent viewpoint in 120 yards.

24.5 .. Stay right at the junction of the Oak Ridge Trail 688A. (The loop can be shortened by taking this route down to Oregon 35. But after all the rough trail riding you shouldn't deny yourself the many miles of smooth, fast downhill riding the longer route affords.)

24.7 .. Cross a road, travel on a smoother tread as you enter woods and soon begin dropping.

25.5 .. Near the base of the lowest power line tower turn right onto a dirt road.

25.6 .. Turn left onto a gravel road.

26.0 .. Turn left onto paved Road 17 and have almost 6.0 miles of fun downhill. There is a cattle guard after 0.4 mile and the road is unpaved between 27.2 and 28.1 miles.

32.5 .. Turn left onto Oregon 35.

33.5 .. Turn left onto Miller Road.

35.5 .. Turn left onto Oregon 35.

36.6 .. Turn right and come to the end of the ride.

East Fork of the Hood River

25 BALD BUTTE LOOP

Difficulty: Moderately hard because of sections of steep trails
Surface: 15.5 miles on paved roads; 1.6 miles on unpaved roads; 3.7 miles on reasonably smooth, wide trails (some of which were formerly roads), except for a 0.5 mile rocky stretch
Distance: 20.8 miles round trip
Elevation gain: 2,500 feet round trip
High point: 3,779 feet
Usually open mid April through early December

Bald Butte is one of the high points on the ridge that forms the east wall of the Upper Hood River Valley. From the top of the treeless expanse below its crest you'll have picture-perfect views over verdant orchards to Mounts Hood, St. Helens, Rainier and Adams. If you consider heading down trails to be the best part of mountain biking, you can retrace your route instead of having an effortless, fun coast back on a paved road. Those wanting a longer loop could combine the route to Bald Butte with part or all of No. 24.

Follow Oregon 35 either 14 miles south from the White Salmon-Government Camp Exit 64 off I-84 just east of Hood River or 26.6 miles east and north from the junction of Oregon 35 and U.S. 26 to the Hood River Ranger Station on the west side of the highway. This is 0.4 mile south of the community of Mt. Hood. Park in the open area to the south of the building (don't take up spaces in front of the station).

00.0 .. Turn left (north) onto Oregon 35, which has an adequate shoulder.
01.1 .. Turn right onto Miller Road.
03.1 .. Turn right onto Oregon 35.
04.0 .. Turn right onto paved Pine Mont Road, which becomes Forest Road 17.
05.9 .. Turn right onto an unpaved, unsigned road and after a short, steep climb travel at a gentle grade.
06.1 .. Come to a fork and follow the signed Surveyors Ridge Trail that is very steep for only the first several yards and soon merges with a narrow, old road bed.
06.4 .. At a crest with a sign stay straight (right) where a road heads downhill. Except for a few short respites, the grade is very steep. However, the surface is firm, so strong riders with light weight bikes will find it entirely rideable. At 7.1 miles level off for a longer stretch and go through a clearcut.
07.3 .. Turn right and in a short distance climb briefly to another level stretch.
07.5 .. Turn right at a junction and continue at a gentle grade through meadowy areas. After a brief downhill stretch, at 8.2 miles begin about 0.4 mile of steep, rocky uphill, which most people will have to walk. As compensation, the views along the middle portion of this stretch are superb. Come to the open summit area at 8.9 miles and contour across it. The recommended stopping point is at 9.0 miles just before a steep downhill stretch. Descend to the west for 50 feet or so for a view directly down to your starting point. You can look across the valley to Mt. Defiance (No. 28), Indian Mountain (No. 26) and Waucoma Ridge (refer to No. 27) and south to Gunsight Ridge (No. 14).

To continue the loop, descend steeply along the road and then ride on a smoother surface and at a more reasonable grade to a gate at 9.6 miles. Be sure to close it after you've gone through. Continue down along the road to the lowest of the four power line towers. The signed Surveyors Ridge trail continues to the south.

09.8 .. Turn left at the base of the lowest power line tower and follow the level dirt road to the east.
09.9 .. Turn left onto a gravel road.
10.3 .. Turn left onto paved Road 17 and start that free ride. Note there's a signed cattle guard after 0.4 mile. The 0.9 mile unpaved section between 11.5 and 12.4 miles has a very good surface. At 14.9 miles pass the road you turned onto at 5.9 miles on the way in.
16.8 .. Turn left onto Oregon 35.
17.7 .. Turn left onto Miller Road.
19.7 .. Turn left onto Oregon 35.
20.4 .. Stay straight on Oregon 35 at the community of Mt. Hood.
20.8 .. Turn right into the ranger station.

Cyclist on summit of Bald Butte

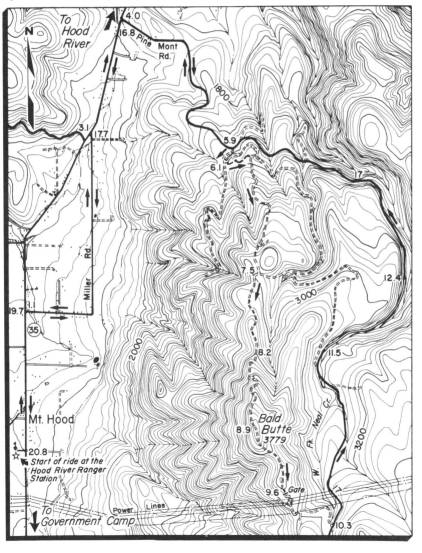

26 INDIAN MOUNTAIN

Difficulty: Moderately easy
Surface: 0 mile on paved roads; 3.9
miles on unpaved roads with
good to fair surfaces except for
0.6 mile along a rocky section;
0.1 mile on a steep trail
Distance: 4 miles one way
Elevation gain: 1,270 feet; 350 feet loss
High point: 4,900 feet
Usually open July through mid October

This ride begins at the saddle above
Wahtum Lake and heads south and west
(No. 27 also begins here, but heads north)
for 3.1 miles to the nose of a big, open ridge
that wouldn't be out of place in the Colo-
rado Rockies. From here you'll have impressive views north over portions of the
Columbia River Gorge to Mounts St.
Helens, Rainier and Adams and then from
the former lookout site on Indian Mountain you'll balance that with scenes south
to Mt. Hood and east to the Hood River
Valley. The area is a favorite of huckleberry
pickers during the second half of August.
For a longer ride you could explore the few
short spurs that take off from the main
road.

If you're approaching on I-84, take the
West Hood River Exit 62 and after 1.2
miles turn right, following a sign to Hospital, Odell and Parkdale. Continue following signs to Odell for 5.1 miles and then
stay right, as indicated by the sign to
Tucker Park. After 6.4 miles keep right
again, drop past the mill at Dee and 0.3
mile from the fork turn left, following the
sign to Lost Lake. Stay on Lost Lake Road
No. 13 for 4.9 miles to the signed road to
Wahtum Lake that takes off at a shallow
angle on your right. After 4.4 miles stay
right and continue on paved road 1310
another 6.1 miles to its end at Wahtum
Lake Campground.

If you're approaching from the west on
Oregon 35, follow it 23 miles from its
junction with U.S. 26 to the road to

Parkdale, just north of the 80 milepost.
After 2.3 miles, turn left, 0.6 mile farther
stay right on the main road at the north
end of Parkdale, continue another 5.1 miles
to the junction above the mill at Dee and
turn left.

Note that the shortest approach from
the Portland area is over Lolo Pass, but
this involves driving on 3.5 miles of
unpaved, rough road on the north side of
the Pass. Take U.S. 26 for 0.3 mile east of
the 42 mile post at the community of Zigzag and turn north on East Lolo Pass
Road. Twenty miles from U.S. 26 stay
right at the junction of the road to Lost
Lake and 2.9 miles farther turn sharply
back to the left onto the signed road to
Wahtum Lake.

00.0 .. Cycle uphill to the west on Road
660, following the sign to Scout Lake and
Indian Springs.

00.5 ..Stay right at the junction of Road
661 down to Scout Lake, which you soon
can see.

01.1 ..Stay right at the junction of Road
No. 662 and begin descending along a
more rustic and fun road that is narrower
and not graveled. Have the first of those
good views to the north at 1.6 miles. At 1.8
mile resume climbing.

02.4 ..Stay straight (left) where a road
heads down to the right to Indian Springs.

02.8 ..Stay right at a fork and in less than
0.1 mile come to an immense berm. Although it's no problem to get around going
in, it's even easier on the way back. Continue along the road for almost 0.2 mile to
the crest of the ridge. Tanner Butte is the
hulk nearby to the northwest and, like all
the terrain below, is in the Columbia Wilderness. The road, now No. 2030, continues along the west side of the ridge but,
unfortunately, it's so rocky it isn't worth
exploring.

03.1 ..Turn left and follow a faint old road
up the broad ridge crest. The surface is
very rocky for the first 0.6 mile. At 3.7
miles enter woods where the surface becomes much smoother.

03.9 ..Come to the end of the road and
begin climbing steeply on a trail that starts
from the northeast side of the little turnaround.

04.0 ..Reach the summit. The high point
above the Upper Hood River Valley with
the lone tree in the middle of the grassy
slope is Bald Butte (No. 25).

View from Waucoma Ridge

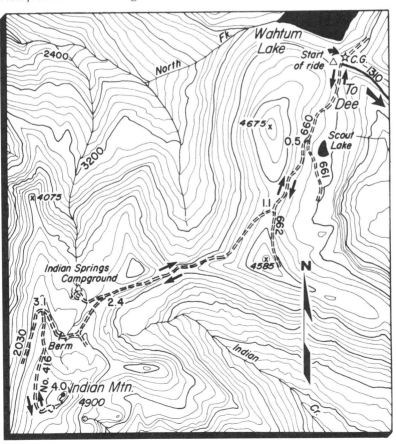

27 RAINY-WAHTUM TRAIL

Difficulty: Hard
Surface: 0 mile on paved roads; 5.7
miles on old roadbed that is
about one-half reasonably firm
rocks and one-quarter each
loose rocks or reasonably
smooth; 0 mile on trails
Distance: 5.7 miles one way
Elevation gain: 665 feet; loss 400 feet
High point: 4,480 feet
Usually open July through October

This fun, but demanding, ride from Wahtum to Rainy Lakes follows an abandoned road along high Waucoma Ridge that forms a portion of the boundary between the Columbia River Gorge and the Hood River Valley. Actually, the route would most accurately be described as a troad: Too wide to be a proper trail, but with sections much too narrow and rough to be passable by any conventional vehicle—in other words, ideal for mountain bikes.

If you're approaching on I-84, take the West Hood River Exit 62 and after 1.2 miles turn right, following a sign to Hospital, Odell and Parkdale. Continue following signs to Odell for 5.1 miles and then stay right, following the sign to Tucker Park. After 6.4 miles stay right again, drop past the mill at Dee and 0.3 mile from the fork turn left, following the sign to Lost Lake. You'll see Road 2810 to the right goes to Rainy Lake but, unlike the one to Wahtum Lake, it is not paved the entire distance. Follow Lost Lake Road No. 13 for 4.9 miles to the signed road to Wahtum Lake that takes off at a shallow angle on your right. After 4.4 miles stay right on paved Road 1310 and continue for another 6.1 miles to its end at Wahtum Lake Campground.

If you're approaching from the west on Oregon 35, follow it 23 miles from its junction with U.S. 26 to the road to Parkdale, just north of the 80 mile post. After 2.3 miles turn left, 0.6 mile farther stay right on the main road at the north end of Parkdale, continue another 5.1 miles

to the junction above the mill at Dee and turn left.

Note that the shortest approach from the Portland area is over Lolo Pass, but this involves driving on 3.5 miles of extremely rough, washboarded and unpaved road on the north side of the Pass. If you want to try it, follow U.S. 26 for 0.3 mile east of the 42 mile post at the community of Zigzag and turn north on East Lolo Pass Road. Twenty miles from U.S. 26 stay right at the junction of the road to Lost Lake and 2.9 miles farther turn sharply back to the left onto the signed road to Wahtum Lake.

00.0 .. Head north along unpaved Road 670 and in a couple of hundred feet come to a gate. Have a short downhill stretch and then begin climbing along the heavily wooded slope. You'll have occasional glimpses of Wahtum Lake below. All along the ride the several trailheads you pass on the west and northwest are closed to bicycles because they are in the Columbia Wilderness.

02.4 .. Come to an open area. The building that once stood here was an old guard station. The Anthill Trail that heads south back to Wahtum Lake just before the clearing is good for cycling for the first 0.4 mile but then becomes rocky, very narrow and occasionally overgrown. So, staying on the road is recommended on the return. Cross the clearing and a berm and continue northeast on the road. Have a steep, rocky stretch to excellent viewpoints at 2.7 and 3.1 miles with sightings of Mounts Hood and St. Helens and the Herman Creek drainage. Except for almost 0.3 mile of level, the route is mostly downhill from here to the turnaround point. Although the views continue, the road is rocky and rough until the 3.3 mile point where the panoramas are exchanged for a very smooth surface, at least relatively speaking. Have that level stretch between 4.0 and 4.3 miles and then resume dropping, passing an old shed on your left at 4.5 miles. Begin having easy little ups and downs 0.4 mile before coming to the turnaround point.

05.7 .. East end of the Rainy-Wahtum Trail.

The 0.3 mile trail to Rainy Lake begins from the north side of the turnaround but immediately enters the Columbia Wilderness, so bicycles are prohibited. However, the lake is worth the short walk.

Rainy Lake

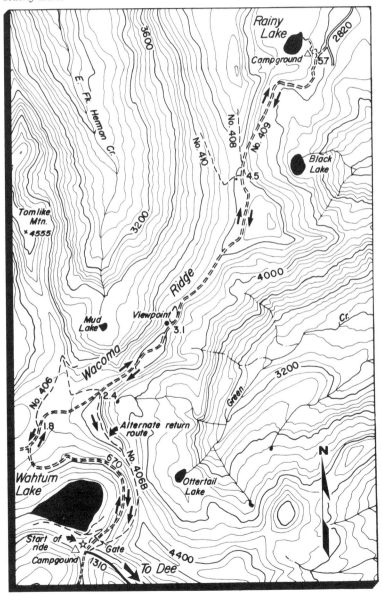

28 MT. DEFIANCE

Difficulty: Moderately hard
Surface: 0 mile on paved roads; 4.2 miles on unpaved roads that are eroded, rocky or steep; 0 mile on trails
Distance: 4.2 miles one way
Elevation gain: 1,800 feet; loss 50 feet
High point: 4,959 feet
Usually open July through mid October

Mt. Defiance is the highest point in the Columbia River Gorge and the view from its summit is appropriately far-ranging, particularly to the east over the Hood River Valleys and beyond into central and eastern Oregon. This is the perfect ride when you feel like following roads that are going to fight back. With the exception of a 0.5 mile stretch at the start, the roads are either eroded, rough, covered with loose rocks or, for the final 0.3 mile, steep. What makes this all a fun challenge, instead of just a challenge, is that they are never steep and rough at the same time. Additionally, the stretches of really hard riding

add up to only about 1.0 mile, which isn't all that far to have to push a bike, if it even comes to that.

Take I-84 to the West Hood River Exit 62. Turn right at the end of the exit and immediately turn right again on Country Club Road. After 3.3 miles turn right at a T-junction, 0.2 mile farther curve left on the main road and in 1.0 mile curve left again, still on Country Club Road. After another 0.7 mile stay right and immediately stay right again, following the sign to Green Point and Kingsley Road. In 0.4 mile turn left onto Kingsley Road, after 1.4 miles come to the end of the pavement and continue another 4.7 miles to possibly unidentified Kingsley Campground and park here. (About 0.5 mile before you come to the campground stay right on the main road where a route heads left past a clearcut.)

00.0 .. Ride down the road for .08 mile to the northeast shore of Upper Green Point Reservoir and pedal across the dam.

00.3 .. Climb the several yards up from the west end of the dam and turn right onto a road. Climb briefly and then travel mostly on the level in woods next to the meadowy area between the Upper and Lower Reservoirs.

00.9 .. Turn left where the road forks.

01.6 .. Stay left where the road forks in a little clearcut and in a short distance begin climbing more noticeably.

02.1 .. Cross a road, continuing in the same direction, and negotiate a deep berm.

02.4 .. Stay left on the road at a fork. The trail that veers off to the left from the road is fun riding, but it ends at another road in a couple of tenths mile.

02.9 .. Keep right onto the "main" road to the summit. Note this junction, so you don't miss it on the return. For the next 0.8 mile the surface is of loose rocks but the grade isn't too severe, then there's a 0.2 mile stretch of smooth, gentle travel before the final stretch that possesses considerably more stable rocks, but is very steep.

04.2 .. Come to the big summit area and the microwave installation there. You'll need to walk to both the far south and far west sides to enjoy all the views. Most cyclists will consider Trail No. 413 that heads north from the summit area, crosses the road and then meets it again below the first switchback to be too rocky and rooty for fun riding.

64

Wind Mountain and Columbia River Gorge

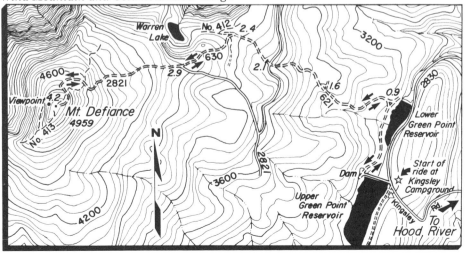

29 HOOD RIVER MOUNTAIN LOOP

Difficulty: Moderately hard, because of distance
Surface: 6.9 miles on paved roads; 16.2 miles on mostly good unpaved roads; 0.8 mile on excellent trails
Distance: 23.9 miles round trip; side trip to a viewpoint would add a total of 0.8 mile; side loop would add 3.3 miles
Elevation gain: 3,100 feet round trip; 440 feet additional for the side loop
High point: 2,700 feet
Usually open May through November

Hood River Mountain forms the east wall of the Lower Hood River Valley and this loop passes expanses of open fields and other exceptionally scenic terrain that might not be expected up there. In addition to enjoying views down onto the Valley and across to Mounts Hood and Adams, you'll be cycling amidst some of those famous orchards.

Because of a fun stretch of downhill trail riding, you're encouraged to begin the optional side loop from the 4.0 mile point and then re-ride the section of road between the saddle at 2.8 miles and the 4.0 mile point. Note that in 1989 there were no Private Property signs on that loop or on the trail cut-off at 7.7 miles. Of course, do not take these—or any—routes if you do encounter closure signs.

Drive on I-84 to the White Salmon-Government Camp Exit 64 just east of Hood River, turn right at the end of the exit, immediately turn right again and take Oregon 35 for 0.7 mile to the road to Panorama Point. Turn left, after 1.5 miles turn right and drive the final 0.2 mile to the Point. Rest rooms are available at the little park here.

00.0 .. Cycle back down the spur road.
00.2 .. Turn right onto East Side Road.
00.6 .. Turn left onto Old Dalles Drive. Come to the end of the pavement at 1.4 miles and continue up at a moderately steep grade.
02.8 .. At the saddle stay straight where a gated, paved road heads left up to a microwave installation. (If you want to climb the trail portion of the optional loop, turn right onto a dirt road at the saddle and after about a hundred feet turn right onto a path. Stay right at a fork after 0.6 mile.)
02.85 Stay right at a fork just beyond the saddle.
04.0 .. Look for an unsigned dirt road on your right. To visit the best viewpoint on the ride follow this side road 0.4 mile, turn left onto a spur and follow it a couple of hundred feet to an overlook. To make the big side loop, follow the road north along the crest. After 0.7 mile the bed narrows to an excellent cycling trail. Descend for 1.0 mile, staying left at a fork about half way down, to the saddle at 2.8 miles.

From the 4.0 mile point continue along the main road and then at 5.6 miles curve left and abruptly begin traveling in woods along a narrower, smoother road.
06.4 .. Stay left where a rough spur heads up to the right.
07.6 .. Stay left at a fork.
07.7 .. Turn right onto an obvious, but unsigned trail. (If this route has been posted as closed, return to the fork at 7.6 miles and take the other (north) branch, which was not ridden by the authors.) After 0.1 mile veer right onto an old road that narrows back to an excellent trail in another 0.1 mile.
08.5 .. Turn left onto a road (the one you would be on if you took the northerly fork at 7.6 miles) at the end of a short, steep descent. From 8.9 to 9.2 miles have the only stretch of steep, rutted road on the entire ride.
09.2 .. Stay left (straight) at a fork in a clearcut and eventually curve right (east).
10.8 .. Turn right (south) onto a better road and alternate between climbing and level stretches.
13.8 .. Stay straight (right) where a road angles back to the left and 0.4 mile farther begin over 6.0 miles of downhill.
15.0 .. Turn right at a T-junction onto a wider road (unsigned, but Fir Mountain Road) and after 3.4 miles begin traveling on pavement.
20.3 .. Turn right onto East Side Road.
23.7 .. Turn left onto the spur to Panorama Point.
23.9 .. End of ride.

Summit of Hood River Mountain

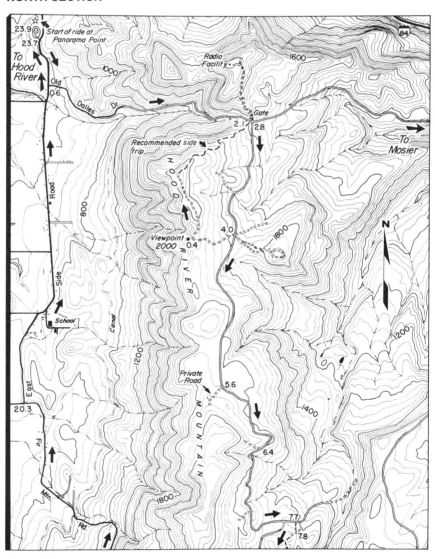

SOUTH SECTION

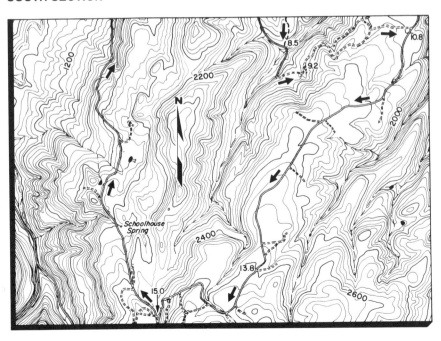

30 MOSIER TUNNEL

Difficulty: Easy
Surface: 5.1 miles on paved roads; 0 mile on unpaved roads; 0 mile on trails
Distance: 5.1 miles one way
Elevation gain: 450 feet (almost all gained along the first 0.9 mile); 100 feet loss
High point: 520 feet
Usually open February through December

This charming ride that begins at Hood River and heads southeast along a section of the original Columbia River Highway is perfect for very young cyclists or anyone absolutely new to mountain biking and having trepidations about it all. Adults who won't tolerate any climbing and those with children who aren't ready to ride in traffic, no matter how light, can begin at the gate at 1.5 miles. Since the route is paved the entire distance, even persnickety road bikers won't be offended. However, opportunities for off-paved road riding are plentiful from several points along the old highway.

Unfortunately, the tunnel at the turn-around point was filled-in with rock during construction of the freeway, but the views on the way there and back are excellent. Particularly engrossing are the barge traffic on the river and the railroad traffic beside it. The trade-off for doing this ride from late fall through early spring (excluding times when the road is snow and/or ice covered) is, although the scene won't be as lushly vegetated, you'll be able to see more because the leaves will be off the deciduous trees that line portions of the north side of the road.

Drive on I-84 to the White Salmon-Government Camp Exit 64 just east of Hood River. Turn right at the end of the exit and then right again, in 0.4 mile come to a 4-way stop and park in the big open area comprising the southeast corner of this intersection. If you're planning to begin from the gate, turn left and drive along the route described below.

00.0 .. Cycle east up winding Old Columbia River Road.

00.7 .. Stay left and continue up, but at a considerably more gentle grade, for another 0.1 mile before traveling on the level for 0.4 mile. Have a final, easy 0.3 mile climb to the gate.

01.5 .. Go around the gate. (Note that it can be opened by people with permits, so you may encounter vehicles, but, presumably, the drivers are aware of pedestrians and cyclists on the road and are proceeding accordingly.) Although it's hardly perceptible, you'll be climbing for 2.9 miles beyond the gate and then gently descending for the final 0.7 mile to the end of the road. Two-tenths mile from the gate pass a grassy road that heads downhill, the first of several opportunities for unpaved (and steeper) explorations. The towns you'll soon be able to see across the river are White Salmon and Bingen. At 2.9 miles come to the first example of those attractive rock guard rails that grace portions of the Old Highway.

Between 3.2 and 3.6 miles travel through a little valley formed by a ridge that separates the Old Highway from the river. At the east end of this valley come to two adjacent roads that head down to a large bench that is good for mountain biking. A bit farther along the paved road you'll have views back to this area, so you have the option of previewing the terrain. Beyond the sign that marks the end of State maintenance at 4.0 miles the road becomes increasingly narrow and moss-enchroached—i.e. more fun. Two-tenths mile from the sign go over a very small berm—the only one on the ride—and 0.1 mile farther at the high point of the ride come to an exceptionally good viewpoint up and down the Columbia River. At 4.7 miles pass another road on your left that you could explore.

05.1 .. Come to the end of the road. Walk a hundred yards along a rocky path to reach the entrance arch of the most westerly of several tunnels that originally were along this stretch of highway.

70

Columbia River from the Old Highway

31 WASCO BUTTE LOOP

Difficulty: Moderate
Surface: 6.2 miles on paved roads; 13.3
miles on good, never steep
unpaved roads; 0 mile on trails
Distance: 19.5 miles round trip
Elevation gain: 2,300 feet
High point: 2,346 feet
Usually open late February through
November

From Mosier this ride climbs past cherry orchards and then alternates between traversing open slopes, which provide far-ranging views, and ones covered with the oak forests so typical of the area. Most of the ride back is along a different route, so you'll get to see more of the region, which is far more complex, topographically, than you might expect. The two prime times to make this ride are in May when the fruit trees are in bloom and in early October when their leaves have turned. Be reminded that the eastern end of the Columbia River Gorge can be very hot in summer.

Drive on I-84 to the Mosier Exit 69, turn right at the end of the exit and continue 0.3 mile to a place for parking on your left (north) across from the base of Washington Street and the Mosier Market.

00.0 .. Head south up Washington Street.
00.06 Turn left onto Third Ave.
00.7 .. Stay straight (left) at the junction of Mosier Creek Road on the route that by here has become signed as State Road and immediately cross a bridge.
00.8 .. Turn right at the other end of the bridge onto Carroll Road. NOTE THAT THERE IS A DANGEROUS GRATE WITH AN OPEN GRID AT THIS TURN.

00.9 .. Stay right on Carroll Road at a fork. If you make the recommended loop, you'll be returning along Dry Creek Road that heads left here. Begin climbing noticeably past those promised orchards.
02.7 .. Turn right. You'll be able to see the top of Mt. Hood from here. In several hundred yards the pavement ends, but the grade eases considerably and is never again as steep.
03.5 .. Stay left, continuing to follow signs to American Adventure, climb a bit more noticeably and then resume the moderate grade.
04.3 .. Stay right at the entrance to American Adventure and continue traversing along the west facing side of the ridge.
05.8 .. Stay right. If you intend to make the recommended loop note this junction because you'll be taking the road to the left on the way back.
06.4 .. Stay left (uphill) at a fork and traverse above a farm. After several tenths mile travel at an easy roller coaster grade pass more open farmland and then begin another stretch in an oak forest.
07.6 .. Turn left onto a possibly unsigned road in another clear area just before the main route drops over the other side of the ridge. This is one of those rare rides where the grade keeps getting easier, instead of steeper, the closer you get to the high point.
08.0 .. Stay right at a small radio tower.
08.1 .. Stay left. All these roads not taken are obviously possibilities for future rides.
08.2 .. Come to the summit with its attendant electronic paraphernalia. Not surprisingly, a fire lookout once stood here.
10.6 .. Retrace your route to the junction at 5.8 miles and turn right. It's all downhill from here, initially along oak covered slopes and then past ever more frequent houses. Although you're only one ridge east of the route you took up, the scenery is markedly different.
13.1 .. Turn left onto Dry Creek Road.
16.0 .. Stay straight (left) on Dry Creek Road at the junction of Morgensen Road. The pavement resumes at this intersection.
18.6 .. Stay right at the junction of Carroll Road, the route you followed up.
18.7 .. Turn left onto State Road.
19.4 .. Turn right onto Washington Street.
19.5 .. End of ride.